Building work at Cologne (15th Cent.)

This interesting illustration is reproduced from a hand-tinted wood-block in *Die Cronica van der Hilliger Stat Coellen*, printed at Cologne in 1499 by J. Koelhoff, the younger, a rare and early book printed in Gothic type. The master-mason, in gown and cap, stands on the left side of the picture and holds a small square in his left hand: near him is a labourer carrving the barrel-head type of mortar hod. Two masons are shown working with mallets or hammers and chisels. At the bottom right-hand corner is a labourer mixing mortar with a hoe-like tool, and the bed containing the mortar has planked sides. A crane with a wheel and pincer-form grips is shown on one of the buildings, and the scaffold appears to be supported by long standards only, without cross-pieces, and it has a very unusual stair-way leading to its upper level.

(Acknowledgement is gratefully made to Mr. F. G. Friehold, of London, for permission to reproduce this illustration from the volume now in his possession)

THE
MEDIAEVAL BUILDER
AND HIS METHODS

FRANCIS B. ANDREWS

DOVER PUBLICATIONS, INC.
Mineola, New York

Bibliographical Note

This Dover edition, first published in 1999, is an unabridged republication of the work originally published in Vol. XLVIII, for the year 1922, of *Transactions and Proceedings of the Birmingham Archaeological Society* (Birmingham, England). This edition also includes "Further Notes on the Mediaeval Builder," first published circa 1928.

Library of Congress Cataloging-in-Publication Data

Andrews, Francis.
    The mediaeval builder and his methods / Francis B. Andrews.
        p.   cm.
    "Unabridged republication of the work originally published in Vol. XLVIII, for the year 1922, of Transactions and proceedings of the Birmingham Archaeological Society (Birmingham, England)"– T.p. verso.
    Includes bibliographical references.
    ISBN 0-486-40672-5 (pbk.)
    1. Building–Europe–History.   2. Architecture, Medieval–Europe. I. Title.
TH17.A5   1999
690'.094'0902–dc21   98-48800
                                                                        CIP

Manufactured in the United States of America
Dover Publications, Inc., 31 East 2nd Street, Mineola, N.Y. 11501

Forenote

THE expression of very kind appreciation by various friends is the warrant for this further publication of my notes on *The Mediaeval Builder*, which have already appeared in the pages of the *Transactions* of the Birmingham Archaeological Society.

The subject and its manifold ramifications have interested me for many years, and my general notes have accumulated far in excess of those here printed. I cannot expect that the arguments I advance in some of the sections will be altogether accepted by every reader, but I have endeavoured to set forth quite frankly the bases on which the conclusions rest, and can only trust that if they do not always convince they will at least give interest.

I acknowledge with gratitude the help and counsel of many friends and the courtesies extended to me at the British Museum; and from the priceless collection of manuscripts thereat some of the illustrations are now reproduced for the first time.

FRANCIS B. ANDREWS.

Contents

List of Plates

The Mediaeval Builder and his Methods

by FRANCIS B. ANDREWS, F.S.A., F.R.Hist.S.

IN mediaeval times the builders worked by slow and laboured means. They followed general rules laid down by revered traditions. Practice in design in later periods was but that to which thoughtful evolution had led from the custom of earlier work. Building with safety was learned in the often hard school of experience, and out of their failures wisdom became sorrowfully known. Work was commenced frequently—if not usually—before anything more than a general idea of the ultimate end had been foreseen, and constructive problems were attempted in the early days with but little knowledge of what would probably be the final statical result. The main lines of a building enterprise having been determined, the decorative and structural details of it were left, more or less, to the moment of their need. Sometimes a piece of work was repeated because it was liked or deemed successful, and at other times use was deliberately made of the successes of others.[1]

This subject—*the builder of mediaeval times*—is a long and difficult one, full of complications and of conflicting evidences, and the records—such as there are—are often capable of more than one interpretation. The men of those days are in no way comparable with those of present experience. They approached their work in so fundamentally different a manner—the one, more from the love of it ; the other, more because of its rewards. Therefore they can only be considered on their own grounds and in relationship to their own day, and clear knowledge of it and of them is hard to come by, and being found is harder still to work up into any sort of sequent story. It was the work itself—finished and in service—that claimed the attention of the contemporary historian, and he had little interest

---

[1] In some cases this was carried so far as to call for positive reference to existing work directing that it was to be taken as a pattern for one about to be set in hand. This was so when, for example, they set down the instructions for the building of Walberswick Church tower (Suffolk) : *R.I.B.A. Journal,* 1901, p. 395.

Or again : the chapel of Windsor, which was to be roofed and ' made after the manner of the new work at Lichfield ' : Hope, *Windsor Castle.*

to make mention of the workers by whose skill and patience the building had come into being—for after all they had but worked as their custom was, and that was not a notable thing that it should be recorded!

This absence of record may be further explicable in the general fact that these building men were just doing ordinary work as they knew it ; it is very doubtful if they ever set out with any idea of doing a great and notable thing or one privately inspired by any name to be made in the success of it. Possibly, even probably, they did not recognize their work as being beautiful—certainly not in the terms in which it is valued to-day. Their work was largely unconscious and free from mere ambition, and the workmen did not note the absence of the chronicler's comment. It was work as work was elsewhere. In broad terms it was all up to an accepted standard and tradition which was attained by obedience to rule and the quiet sequence of evolution, and therefore nothing was specially present to require mention or praise ; nor was it any more necessary then to write the names of the workers in history than it is to-day to record those who have been honest in the labours of the trade of their choice. Hence the record of the mediaeval builder and his fellows is very largely wanting, at least in English record.

 ' Throughout antiquity, the work of the painter, the sculptor, and the architect seems to have been taken for granted. People did not discuss it or even think about it because they could not conceive of it other than it was. And it seems to have been much the same in mediaeval times. A few names of master-builders have reached us ; we know so little about them that we do not even know how they set out their buildings or who were their sculptors and how they carved their images. My impression is that the artists and the craftsmen were still regarded as men of little account. The change came with the Renaissance. Up to that date artists *had* been humble persons working among their fellows and with their fellows, on the same plane and without any claim to exceptional merit. With the Renaissance they emerge as individuals. That movement started from above, from the scholars and intellectuals, and worked downward till it reached the artist and the craftsman. The noble patron appears upon the scene to run his artist like a race-horse against his rival's entry, the arts became conscious of themselves, and henceforward the initiative of the individual was to take the place of the pre-destined course of immemorial tradition, a process which has ended in the alarming results of latter-day Art.' [1]

[1] Sir Reginald Blomfield, *Address to the Birmingham and Midland Institute*, 1924.

It will be well to admit at once that, although long and careful search has been made, and a great mass of notes collected, all cannot be said here, nor is it hoped to bring the inquiry about these builders and their affairs to a final and satisfactory conclusion, but rather to set forth some of the leading facts anew and to draw such inferences from them as they appear to admit.[1]   In so doing some fresh views of the subject may perhaps be obtained, or at least help given in reconciling opinions that have already been expressed, some of which seem to be in conflict.

For convenience in dealing with the various branches of the subject, it has been divided into sections:

§ 1. On the General Subject

That the mediaeval builder frequently began operations with little else pre-arranged than the general scheme of the building, may be quite safely affirmed.   They appear to have had but few drawings[2] of any sort, and those that they had, when compared with the work they allege to have forecast, are difficult to reconcile or even understand because of their crudity and incompleteness.

The working relationships of mediaeval times were very different to those of modern custom.   The motives of their craft-guilds and trade confraternities were inspired by far higher ideals than those of the trade unions of to-day.   They were also under a very different sort of control—nor, indeed, have the latter any roots or originations in the former, despite the frequent averments of interested modern exponents thereof.   They were absolutely dissimilar—

---

[1] See Authorities, Appendix II, p. 97.
[2] See later, 'Notes on Drawings', § 8, pp. 80–8.

in aim, end, and management—and they bear no sort of likeness to one another.

There was indubitably a great love of the work in those days : love of it for its own sake, and a still greater love of it for its ultimate purpose. In this the Church was very largely involved and very fully participated—too fully at times and so much so that its leaders occasionally felt forced to intervene with the firmest of interdictions.[1] The better class of workers were actuated by high ideals in their craft, and conflicts between capital and labour were practically absent in the earlier years and comparatively little known in the later, at least in anything like the bitterness of form in which they have been expressed in days of current experience.[2]

Good workmanship dominated everything else ; the good work-man was paid, clothed, and honoured, and has left behind him —if not his name—at least the glory of true and loving service, and in so much it is all far removed from even the best work of to-day. Of the mere competition of prices of modern idea there was none. ' To build with beauty and design with truth ' and in obedience to tradition, were the great purposes of their efforts, and they built as it never has been done since and probably never will be done again.

There is, however, some danger that this statement about working for the love of it may be very easily overstressed, and has been, at least as regards the general workman's point of view. They cannot all have been idealists—they certainly were not ; toil after all was toil then as now, and it is a rare spirit that does not faint under the weariness of the flesh. Besides this there must have been some amongst them whose hearts were more or less distant. There are

[1] ' This glorying in their churches and their over-costly and superfluous buildings called out the rigours of the Cistercian Order. On one occasion, 1192, two abbots were punished by the General Chapter for such excess. Even painting and carving was prohibited, and still later (1240) carved reredoses forbidden. Stone towers, bells more heavy than five hundredweight, and many other matters came within these and later interdictions. The architects had to seek beauty in the simplest possible elements ; nor did they fail to find it— of which Fountains is a notable example.' G. C. Coulton, *Five Centuries of Religion*, 1923, vol. i.

[2] There was strife enough between the peasant and his lord ; the latter half of the fourteenth century was full of bitter strugglings, and undoubtedly some part of these great troubles in agricultural concerns overflowed in con-flicts in trade and labour of all sorts, but what it is intended to convey here is the almost entire absence of such controversies as the building trade knows to-day in strikes, lock-outs, and the violent disputes stimulated by paid agitators.

records enough of careless workers and even of others who were of a callous—if not a malign—mind toward their work, and the presence of this spirit cannot be obliterated or ignored by emphasizing the fervours of building promoters or the ideals of the better masters whom they employed.

It seems reasonable enough to conclude that while certain of the workers were indeed filled with zeal and laboured in the impulse of it, there was also a contingent—and possibly a substantial contingent—of labourers who were no more than mere wage-workers, who lived by their trade rather than for it and who did not work because of any higher claims, but whose primary object was to receive the present rewards.[1] No period has been, nor will any ever be immune from the discontented worker or free from the greed of the profiteer, and it must be frankly acknowledged that both existed even in the most idealistic periods of art, for art, like all else, has never been altogether and exclusively—' art for art's sake '.

With the true-minded mediaeval worker, however, the ideal persisted, and art progressed, one phase growing quietly and naturally out of a former, growing more beautiful in the earlier stages of development, though ultimately, at the close of the mediaeval period, degenerating in excess and confusion from which there is little sign of resurrection yet in any way worthy to be called glorious. The Renaissance, when it came, was by no means to architecture a rebirth of the old and true craft-spirit or a clarification of the stream of evolution, but was merely a widening of knowledge whereby the art was degraded into a mere purveyance of style as demanded by the caprice of patronage. Intuition was ousted by intellect, and intuition has not yet returned.

So slow indeed were the developments of the art, and so long were the periods that divided any substantial change in architectural form from another, that it is hard to forgive the man who suggested *an attempt to discriminate* them by time divisions—by twelfth-, thirteenth-, fourteenth-, or fifteenth-century periods—and who parcelled them up and labelled them ' styles '.[2] No such discrimination or parcelling is possible at all.

---

[1] This lamentable condition may be inferred as existent in Wyclif's day, when he proclaimed *The grete Sentens of Curs* and said :

'. . . alle newe fraternytes or gildis maad of men semes openly to renne in this curs . . . For thei conspirin togidere that no man of here craft schal take lesse on a day than thei setten, though he schude bi good conscience take moche lesse and noon of hem schal make sade trewe werk to lette othere mennes wynnyng of the craft. . . .' *Select English Works*, T. Arnold, vol. iii.

[2] Which were classified as the *Norman, Early English, Decorated, Perpen-*

Evolution there was—evolution that may be traced so obviously in the many matters of the life and needs of man, certainly applied also to his building work—that art which ever most truly displays his character—the art of his architecture.[1]   And it was the guilds that generally conserved and controlled these developments and that gave intelligent utterance to the stages of their progression. Nearly if not all the trade-crafts, and the accumulating experiences of them, were represented by Guild Companies in the Middle Ages not only in the ' mistery ' of the mason or carpenter's craft, but in all the crafts even down to the capper's ' mistery ' at Coventry.

It has been said by some that England depended on other nations, rather than on her own initiative, for the development of her architecture ; and while evidences of foreign influence can no doubt be produced, they certainly do not suffice for so wide an assertion. It has in fact no substantial continuing truth.   Whatever influence there was, was of early times, was transient, partial and very much localized.   If it be admitted that there are buildings in England that show the influence of alien *motif* in design and decorative detail— and it cannot be denied (nor indeed, that even foreign masters and their workmen came and worked on English buildings in the earlier periods)—still there is no sufficient ground for a general statement that England owes her architectural developments to importations from France or any other country.

Without attempting to trace the previous course of architectural sequence, it may be noted that in early Norman days there were certainly very definite importations of idea.   The *Romanesque* (often,

dicular, and *Debased* styles.   Rickman, an architect some of whose work is yet to be seen in Birmingham, was the first so to do, and M. H. Bloxam, a Warwickshire antiquary, followed in his lead.

' We have been told for nearly a century that there are four periods of English Mediaeval Architecture. . . . But there is no such thing. . . . The whole classification (of styles) is mischievous as well as baseless.   The novice is led to believe that architecture stopped at the end of the four periods, turned over a new leaf and began again *de novo*. . . .'

' Evolution, not a blind and unnatural change. . . . For every change there was a reason.'   *Gothic Architecture*, F. Bond, Pref., p. xx.

[1] ' From Roman to Renaissance the history of Architecture is an unintercepted series of transitions . . . in the fashion in which we study the development of a living being, which from infancy passes to age by a series of insensible transformations without it being possible from one day to another to say where infancy or youth ceases or where age begins.'   Viollet-le-Duc, *Essays*.

' A notable building, indeed any work of art, is not the product of an act of design by some individual genius, it is the outcome of ages of experiment. Lethaby, *Architecture*, p. 206.

but erroneously, called *Norman*) was further developed on the Continent—although it was already existent in crude form in England [1]—and the Norman prelates and bishops and others, being appointed to high official positions in England after its Conquest, naturally brought over with them the ideas of their native country, but these were very shortly modified by the English idea,

> '. . . when transplanted on English soil their offspring . . . quickly outgrew the stature and measure of the parent . . . its greatest triumph and culminating development is in Anglo-Norman England.' [2]

It is probably quite right to say that, except for Westminster,[3] and one or two other special instances, the French influence had become submerged in the English idiom and practically lost to sight after what is known as the *Norman-Transitional* period,[4] and the *Early English* work which emerged from it was wholly the product of the native art and mind.[5] It is very certain that with the disappearance of the round arch, the design-forms on this side of the Channel diverged very definitely from those on the other side. The political changes of the times, no doubt, largely contributed to this condition ; when the miserable and shifty Lackland lost so many of its Continental possessions, England's closer union with France and with French aims and methods was considerably reduced—albeit to England's gain in more than matters of her art—and she struck out along lines of her own.[6]

[1] Saxon work existed before the coming of the Normans and it contained germs at least of the *Romanesque* idea, but with evidences of *Byzantine* influence.

[2] Power, *Lectures to Goldsmiths' Company*, 1907.

[3] Westminster exhibits strong analogies to Rheims, but the details are typically English—this Scott and Lethaby have noted and admit (see their books on Westminster). Amiens also had its influence there.

[4] This and like terms are used for convenience of definition only.

[5] There has been a great deal of controversy on the extent of French influence on the earlier English work. It may also be pointed out that there was certainly a reaction in the indubitable evidence of English influence on the later French *flamboyant* work. This view is also taken by Power in his lectures to the Goldsmiths' Company, see his *Mediaeval Architecture*, vol. i, p. 75.

[6] 'From the Churches alone we might infer the presence of a conquering race . . . the foreign influences are palpable ; the breach with the past of English art is violent and sudden ; the absence of a transitional stage denotes that we are dealing with an importation, not with a natural development. At the same time the new architects, though immigrants, are obviously at their ease. They build slowly, solidly . . . they show the interest of a settler in the conditions of the land which they have overrun. They form a school with developing traditions . . . they make a style which is not purely Norman

But as to the builders—Professor Lethaby says:

'We are unfortunately very much in the dark in England as to the Mediaeval Builder. French and other Continental records give more precise particulars: We know that Rheims, Amiens, and La Sainte Chapelle were the work of men who called themselves masons: we know the wages they received . . . we can visit their burial places. . . . But there is a curious reserve here in England about the " architects " of our English Cathedrals and no general attempt has been made to know the facts . . . vague theories still hold the field. We go on repeating that it is unknown who built the wonders of mediaeval art, or that they were the work of monks, or of travelling free-masons or of a Comacine guild, or they were designed by clerks like Elgar of Dereham, Edward of Westminster, or William of Wykeham.'

and he continues further:

'The main facts . . . are roughly these . . . carpenters, masons, smiths, glaziers, &c., existed in separate or general crafts. . . . These crafts organized the education of the body as a whole . . . the real explanation of mediaeval art is to be found in the fact that craft industry, through its organized guilds, claimed and won an honourable place in life . . . the craftsman would have no lord's man in his guild, and his instinct set him against all handling of goods for profit and brokerage . . . when such a work as a cathedral was going forward a resident master-mason or carpenter was employed as architect (probably the former) to do the work. . . . Designing was mere contrivance, the doing of work in an ordinary way. . . . Cases might be found where some mason recognized as a great master could not be attracted to a new work, but would advise by consultation and by means of rough patterns while the resident mason would work under his advice.'[1]

The general point which it is desired to establish first is that no individual designer *qua* architect was existent and that *per se* he was not necessary.[2] No church or other work was just the outcome of the mind of any single man who had sat down and deliberately designed it and having drawn it then got up and supervised its execution—certainly not in any such sense as it is understood to-day. Such a man was not necessary—the idea of design was already existent when the mason took up his tools, and he knew it and worked

any more than it is Saxon . . .' and Prof. Davis goes on to show how style in building developed into the richer forms of the fifteenth century and fell 'into harmony with the English atmosphere and landscape'. H. W. C. Davis, 'England under the Normans and Angevins', *History of England*, vol. i, pp. 181 et seq.

[1] 'Education in Building', *R.I.B.A. Journal*, 1901, pp. 385 et seq.

[2] '. . . that which we understand by architect did not exist in the Middle Ages—neither the name nor the thing.' Durand, *Cathédrale d'Amiens*, 1901.

to it, carrying forward unconsciously the course of evolution. What was wanted and what was supplied was the man who would work earnestly and honourably and leave, so to speak, the designing to take care of itself. Hence there was no architect to *make* a design —no superior or aloof person above and apart from the workers, save only where the magnitude of the work or the multiplicity of his undertakings made it impossible for the master-mason or master-carpenter to take actual tools in hand and labour with the rest of the workers. In the best periods he was always *of* them— they were called his *socii*—his *fellows*, and he a fellow-worker, but wiser—with a larger hope and a fuller vision.

In later times, however, this began to change—the master no longer worked himself, he took oversight only and walked about in a nice gown and gave directions, and finally in the Renaissance he became a ' professional ' man ! In a sermon of the later Middle Ages is a plaint—' Some work by word alone. For, take notice, in great building there is usually a single master-builder who directs the construction by word alone and seldom does manual labour.' [1]

There seems to be three fairly clear though conflicting opinions current as to the persons who dealt with the building affairs of mediaeval times: (*a*) the first avers that the builders of the Middle Ages were monks (i. e. men of the Church) ; (*b*) the second, that they were lay ' master-masons ' or other trade masters ; and (*c*) the third, that the work was directed and controlled by persons somewhere between the other two, men whose relationships were more or less those of an independent or ' professional ' kind though not quite of the same sort as those of the present day.[2]

Of these three suggestions the argument of this section of the subject will endeavour to confirm the second, modifying it slightly to admit some of the claims of both the first and the third, but chiefly urging that the second most completely satisfies the question.

And then another point arises—one which seeks to account for the widespread parallelism of architectural work, how it comes to be that north, south, east, and west, save for the minor and local divergencies, a common idea or *motif* seems to run through all the phases of mediaeval design. Here guild control has direct application.

---

[1] Quoted by Kingsley Porter in his *Mediaeval Architecture.*

[2] ' There was no such recognized profession as that of architect in the Middle Ages . . . buildings grew rather than were designed. The Bishop must have . . . arranged the general rough plan and the workmen the details, designed and executed as occasion arose under the eye of the foreman or " master ".' *Guide to English Architecture,* Gardner, 1922.

In order to argue these general questions, and beginning with the builders, let it be postulated:

(*a*) That the frequent averment that this or that ecclesiastic built or enlarged an edifice is to be usually understood as meaning that *he set such a scheme in hand*—that he approved or indicated the general lines of the building proposed, or (and most probable of all) that he provided the means whereby it could be carried into effect— but not at all implying that he was the *master* in the matter of its design or was in guild or working relationships with the men. A *master* was probably employed for the purpose (though that is rarely specifically mentioned), and that man (by whatever name he may have been designated—and there were many) was in immediate contact with and responsible for the work.

(*b*) That these *masters* sometimes even entered into contracts for work for which at times they also agreed to find both the materials and the labour, but at other times these were found for them.

(*c*) That both the *master* and the workmen were members in and under the rules of a *guild*, and they were entirely controlled by conditions determined by the craft, irrespective of any particular place or work; that they were sworn to carry out work according to those rules, even down to the moulds and patterns they used (though of course, throughout the kingdom there were slight variants). And further that in connexion with these men there were *lodges* or places of work and rest and of secret conclave.

§ 2. On the Masters in Building-Craft

1. To begin with—on the question whether this somewhat elusive person, ' the master ', is to be found as an official of the Church— it might be argued on a simple question as to whether he could have had available time and be at liberty so to do. How could a cleric find opportunity for such commissions ? Any one in charge of a building work (certainly if it were of any magnitude) would necessarily find his time exclusively occupied by it—for besides generally directing the development of the design there was (at least in the earlier days) the actual work which the ' master ' did with his own hands, as well as the setting-out and superintending the work of others, and still further the time spent in attending craft conferences. Would it have been possible for a churchman— a bishop, an abbot, a prior, or even a sub-officer of a convent—to discharge these duties as well as those of his conventual office ? [1]

[1] ' It could not with any show of probability be contended that fierce soldiers and busy politicians like Bishops Roger of Salisbury and Pudsey of

In their execution also, all building works would have to be carried out in proper compliance with the traditions of trade-craft and according to guild rules. And if it be argued that the church-man's spiritual duties could be performed by proxy, which is doubtful, it is very certain that those of craft mastership could not be so performed—he *must* attend the *lodge*. Nor is it likely that this was attempted in either case, but there is nothing to have prevented an able-bodied monk from being detached by his superior to assist in the building work of his house or church. Indeed this was frequently done, and possibly the experience so gained may have been afterwards used by such an one in the conduct of certain, probably minor, building affairs at a later date.

But it cannot be supposed that, for example, William de Newnton, Abbot of Pershore (1413–50), set to and designed the new bridge over the Avon and put monk-masons, or a self-collected gang of lay-masons, on to the building of it and superintended their work. But the bridge or bridges, for there are three, were built, or are said to have been built, by the Abbot and Convent, needing them because their late abbot, William Upton, had been drowned in crossing the river by boat in flood time. The probable facts of the case were that the Convent, bewailing its loss and fearful of a repetition of the catastrophe, urged its abbot to call in some master bridge-builder and to bid him do the work with all speed, gathering such men and materials as he required for the purpose, the Abbot probably helping him or wholly supplying the latter. The stone in this case must have been fetched from afar, for it is a sandstone, and only a poor sort of limestone is to be found anywhere in the district. The Abbot then provided the monies for its cost and levied a pontage on the passers (obtaining royal leave so to do), and this was probably all he had to do with it as a piece of work, for he had his conventual duties to attend to day by day, and the exacting direction and over-sight of the building of the bridges would have demanded more time than he had to spare and a kind of knowledge in which he had neither training nor experience. Yet the records say he built the bridge!

2. Neither could the cleric have been a craft-master unless he

Durham could have been the personal designers of great cathedrals . . . every-thing tended to prove that the bishops hired the builders and masons . . . there was no doubt that the cleric dictated the general idea . . . but not what we mean by personal design now-a-days.' ' The ground plan having been determined, the masons did the rest.' E. S. Prior, *The Basis of English Gothic Architecture*, a paper read to the Architectural Association, London, Feb. 1901.

had passed through the necessary stages of learning: first a sworn *apprentice*, later, a *journeyman*, and finally a *master* in a duly recognized lodge; failing such the men would not have admitted his authority, nor would he have known how to direct them or their work, not being admitted to congregations, nor having access to the secrets of the craft *loge*, or being able to obtain the moulds and patterns. To argue that all this could be waived is to make nonsense of all the records, traditions, and development in architecture, to say nothing of masonic authority, a body of evidence that cannot be easily gainsaid or lightly set aside.

No church official—strong as the Church was—could arrogate to himself, even at the bidding of a Chapter, any such position. In saying this it is not intended to exclude the possibility that a member of a convent, at some time prior to his admission thereto, might have passed through the accepted craft training,[1] nor that a craftsman might have been admitted to the Church after his services to it as a layman and in reward for his devotion, and so supported the idea that the Church supplied the ' masters '.

3. In the earlier periods no doubt the Church did a good deal of work for herself and set her sons to the labours of it. Up to the twelfth century, and probably well into it, cases can be produced where church officials and monk-masons and carpenters directed building operations and some of them also actually worked therein.[2]

---

[1] But quite to what extent the monastic vow might have collided with the masonic it is a little hard to say ! I have sought for a definite answer to this question in various directions but have not been able to find one.

[2] After the fire at Canterbury in 1057 it is recorded by Eadmer (translating from the Latin freely)—that ' that most energetic and honourable man, Lanfranc, Abbot of Caen, was made Archbishop of Canterbury . . . ' when he came and found ' almost nothing by fire and ruin, he was filled with consternation . . . he pulled down to the ground all that he found of the burnt monastery . . . and having dug out their foundations from under the earth, he constructed in their stead others, which excelled them greatly in beauty and magnitude. He built cloisters, cellarer's office, refectories, dormitories. . . . As for the church, . . . he set about to destroy it utterly and erect a more noble one . . . and in the space of seven years he raised this new church from the very foundations and rendered it almost perfect '.   There is little doubt that Eadmer's omission of any other than the Archbishop's name is due to feelings of major esteem—the master mason being no more than a servant ! See Willis, *Hist. of Canterbury*, 1845.

There is nothing in the above record which would exclude the suggestion that he did the work by employing a master-mason. He certainly employed French workers.

Further: a St. Denis MS., eleventh century, says—' He (the abbot) suffered men (*viri*) who were skilled in architecture ' ; the secular word *viri* would not have been used if clerics had been referred to.

But later and even contemporarily therewith the lay-master was engaged and almost exclusively on the more important enterprises.

The buildings of early times—though later replaced by more ornate and permanent structures—were most frequently of wood,[1] and often of the crudest workmanship and design—fitly attributable to untrained effort, by which indeed they were executed. Such instances as these may be rightly referred to ecclesiastical effort in its zeal to provide the necessary buildings for worship and shelter as the religious pioneers proceeded with their missionary settlements; but the more permanent structures of later days belong to the experience of ' masters ' in building. Professor Simpson considers ' the enormous strides in French design between 1150 and 1220 were due to the advent of the lay-man '.[2]

An interesting evidence of this early timber building is shown in the Anglo-Saxon translation of Matt. vii. 26, 27 : [3]

> ' And æk thæra the gehyrath thas mine word . . . bith gelic tham dysigan man tha *getimbrode* hys hus ofer sand-ceosel . . .'
> [And each of them that (ge)heareth these mine words . . . beeth (ge)like that foolish (dizzy) man that (ge)timbered his house over sand-gravel . . .]

The Anglo-Saxons being a ship-building people used timber for their homes, and stone building was comparatively rare. A note in the Domesday Survey Book which reads ' ibi presbyter et ecclesia lignea ' (Byland, Yorkshire) refers to a timber church.

Prof. Baldwin Browne, describing the procedures in the founding of Ramsey Abbey (Hunts.) says that Bishop Oswald of Worcester visited the site, being known to Alderman Ailwyn who had probably invited his (the Bishop's) counsel, and he promised to send a skilled man from the Monastery at Worcester, one who could direct the building work, and he further said help should be sent from Westbury. Ædnoth, a priest and steward (*dispensator*), was sent, and he gathered workmen together. He first enlarged the timber church and then prepared materials for the new work and it was set in hand. After the building had been generally completed a crack appeared in the central tower, whereupon Alderman Ailwyn being sent for, he called in certain *cementarii*[4] for expert advice, and

---

[1] A.-S. *timbrian* = to build, literally *to timber*, so much was timber the exclusive material for structures which could be called buildings.

[2] *History of Architecture*.

[3] Forshall and Madden's *Anglo-Saxon Gospels*.

[4] The lay-masons are here called in, the work being beyond the skill or knowledge of the monk whose work had failed.

they concluded that it must be taken down, the foundations strengthened and the tower rebuilt ; this was done, and some of the younger monks were employed to help.[1]

4. A similar and equally early account of a building work in France [2] is to be found which relates that in A. D. 1110, Geoffroy, Abbot of the Trinity at Vendôme, lent to Hildebert, Bishop of Le Mans, who was then rebuilding his cathedral, a monk named Jean, who had a reputation of being an excellent master-builder. The record goes on to say that Hildebert was so pleased with the work done that he ignored all the appeals of Geoffroy for the return of Jean.

5. Again, if the ecclesiastics were indeed ' masters ', the question arises : Master in what ?　Master-mason is the *almost exclusive* inference when work is attributed to churchmen.　But what of the other chief workers of whom mention is made over and over again and for whom there was certainly equal need ?　The master-carpenter, the master-plumber, and the masters in other trades. Is it to be concluded that the churchmen were only (if of any) ' masters ' of mason-craft ?　The masonry being done, were the roofs and their coverings, the screens, stalls, and all the other quite important and integral parts of the building turned over to lay-masters or had they no ' masters ' at all ?　And be it carefully borne in mind that there was no one single master who had charge of all : such is quite a modern idea.

6. Then if the Church found the master minds for ecclesiastical work, who did the secular ? [3]　The castles, the bridges, the civil buildings, and the houses ?　These things required equal skill and experience :　these things, too, exhibit the traditional evolutions, though possibly in a less obvious way.

7. It is true that Church work shows most clearly the movements of design, but this is simply because the recognizable features in design are comparatively so few in many of the buildings of lay purpose ;　but that cannot justify a claim that the branch of ecclesiastical mason-craft was separate or distinct from that of lay structures or that there was any such branch or that it was in the hands of the Church.　The truth is that the Church work had more

---

[1] Baldwin Browne, *Arts in Early England*, vol. i, p. 246.　This is an early instance in the twelfth century.

[2] Enlart, *Manuel d'Archéologie française*, i. 62, where two other instances of monk master-builders are given.

[3] It is true that such men as William of Wykeham or Alcock of Worcester did do secular work, but this (certainly in the case of the former) was in their pre-clerical days.

detail and more lavish treatment because it was the Church : more able to provide for the expense and more diligently served because of its appreciation of the arts and its dominance over the minds, if not always over the hearts of the people.

8. And yet again : it must be remembered that of the few and bare records that there are, they are almost exclusively of monastic origin. Now the monkish chronicler was ever anxious to conserve the honour of the Church—he even distorted facts to this end—it was an *ex parte* record in almost every case, and when he was minded to speak of the buildings of his house, he was far more anxious to record their greatness, their beauty, and their glorious service than —to him—the uninteresting details of their erection.[1]   That his Superior had ordered the work, collected the funds for it and perhaps some of the materials, and ultimately blessed it, was not only enough for him—it was paramount ; such a man was the only person to be remembered, and nothing mattered—or practically nothing—about those who had laboured in its design and worked its beauties in lasting stone and timber.[2]   As to the civil work outside the Church, unsought by it and not (at least formally) blessed by its hands—the cloistered historian had nothing whatever to say, nor indeed had hardly any other writer of the times.   Hence, it is easy to account for the general idea that what was done in these things was done by them of the Church, and it was so recorded in general terms, and therefore credit for the act and article of the doing of it at length became attached to churchmen, and the lay-worker was ignored.[3]

Dr. Anton Springer of Bonn, in a learned Latin essay [4] on the subject of *Monastic and Lay Workers of the Middle Ages*, discusses the chief works of Mediaeval Art.   He opines that when the word

[1] 'In spite of Abbé Rocher's pathetic anxiety to claim all the building, writing, teaching, &c., as the direct work of the monks, his documents distinctly imply the contrary. . . . There is no hint that the bell-founder and the two architects mentioned on pp. 111, 113, and 120 of the *Miracles de St. Benoît* (E. Certain, Société de l'histoire de France) were monks ; on p. 319 we find a monk superintending the workmen, but only as a financier ; on p. 327 it is distinctly implied that the builders were all lay folk.' *Five Centuries of Religion*, Coulton, vol. i, p. 252.

[2] 'The abbots staked their self-respect on the beauty of these (cathedral) buildings. They liked their names to be associated with the *opus ædificale* . . . they loved the edifice which was destined to exalt their memory in the eyes of their successors.' *The Middle Ages* (National Hist. of France Series), Fr. Funck-Brentano, p. 215.

[3] 'There is no doubt that the cleric dictated the general ideas . . . but not what we mean by personal design now-a-days.' E. S. Prior., op. cit.

[4] *De Artificibus Monachis et Laicis Medii Aevi*, 1861.

' built ' or ' made ' is used and attached to the former, it more often than not should be construed to mean ' caused to be made ', or ' provided for the building of '.   He cites examples of obvious pertinence, and urges that the greatest caution should be adopted in accepting the names of bishops, abbots, and others as practical craftsmen : that it is necessary to search beyond the first statement of such condition, and that it will probably be found that the inclusion of the name as among the clergy is *subsequent to* the days of practical relationships to building work in any sense as a master-mason. Dr. Springer is by no means wishful to deny to the cloister its due share in the fine arts, but he is insistent, and rightly so, that the lay element, if not exclusive of all other, was in large and dominating majority.   There were indeed great designers occasionally found among the clergy, none less than such men as Bishops Wykeham and Alcock, and to these, in a certain careful sense, the term ' architect ' might possibly be applied.   But most of them had had a previous lay-training, and the work attributed to them generally belongs to their pre-ecclesiastical days.

Mr. Papworth [1] went so far as to say that even great men like Wykeham—who indubitably did a great deal of actual work in his lay days—had in later life and after his elevation to the bishopric his own master-mason, and named William of Wyneford as the man ; in support of this he cites Wyneford's portrait at Winchester College and the directions of the bishop's will, whereas the work is usually attributed to Wykeham himself.

9. And yet again—even if it be but a slender argument—the records often speak of gifts and rewards, by the Crown and by ecclesiastical dignitaries themselves, to master-masons ; gifts of land, of the tenure of houses, of properties, and of monies and even of life pensions.   Such worldly emoluments as those could not have been offered to or accepted by a monk—he would need no land, no house, no pension—his convent found all that his vows permitted him to enjoy—and we do not read anywhere of grants and benefactions to monastic houses in recognition of building services rendered by them or by their inmates.

10. Besides these matters, confusion has no doubt been imported into the case because many of the large ecclesiastical establishments had their own building staffs, and doubtless some of the obedientaries also studied the art. [2]   These departments were important enough

---

[1] *R.I.B.A. Trans.* 1887.

[2] See p. 13, Ædnoth, the man sent by the Bishop of Worcester to Ramsey.

in their skill and recognition to be styled ' schools ' ; at Westminster, Wells, York, Gloucester, St. Albans, and elsewhere, they had them ; [1] and there is little doubt that the abbot or head of the establishment would take or be given the credit for the work they did—certainly of that which they did at home, and so the idea gained currency that such were the actual authors, and the monks the executants of the designs.

At Canterbury, the registers early in the fifteenth century give a list of the *artifices* of the house ; it includes carpenters, tylers, and masons. A little later (1428) the class is styled *lathomi* and included twenty stone-cutters, six layers, two apprentices,[2] and four labourers. In the year following these are referred to again as *lathomi de la Loygge*—which directly evidences the existence of a lodge or in other words a guild or school—but of this later. At York similar and very clear records may be found.[3]

11. Still another factor arises, and that is in the instances where a skilled lay-master was, in honour to his ability, received into the Church spiritual after he had laboured on the Church physical.[4] Cases of this procedure are on record of which William of Wykeham (above mentioned), a most celebrated ' master', had certain benefices conferred on him by the Crown and afterwards was made a bishop ; [5] or Abbot Boyfield of Gloucester, who was a lay-master builder in his earlier years, or Alcock of Worcester, also made a bishop at a later date, may be cited as examples.

12. There are records also of the ' masters' undertaking work by contract. Such procedure must argue their freedom from any sort of outside control, and therefore no such ' master ' could possibly have been a monk or even a lay-clerk. He must have been an independent person able to control his own movements without any sort of trammel or overlordship. Evidently such a ' master' could not have been a churchman.

[1] See Smith's *Antiquities of Westminster* ; *York Fabric Rolls* (Surtees Society), &c., &c.

[2] An apprentice infers a *master* and certainly, therefore, a ' loge ', and this is actually mentioned in a later record ; the apprentice could hardly be of the brethren of the house. How could he take the oaths of secrecy in the lodge ?

[3] See *York Fabric Rolls*, 1522, Surtees Society, vol. xxxv (1858).

[4] If such were done, and it seems to have been, it is not easy to see how the lodge secrets were dealt with ; possibly some special dispensation operated to conserve the pledges given under oath by the entrant to holy orders.

[5] In evidence of this Wyclif's complaint at the time of Wykeham's appointment may be cited : ' They wullen not present a clerk able of God's word and a holy ensample, but a kitchen clerk or a penny clerk, or one wise in building castles or other worldly doings.' However discourteous and in a measure untrue this may have been, it assists the present argument.

13. And a last point is the almost total absence of mention in records of any ' architect ' as such—a superior person with authority over and above the master-mason [1] (whether designated *cementarius* or *lathomus*). Surely had such existed, there would, even in the scanty records that remain, have been mention of them somewhere. But the fact remains that while general terms express the directions of the Church and its officials, it is the master-mason alone whose name is associated with the actual execution of the works as the responsible person.[2]

To take a few actual records by way of illustration :

i. In 1077, Robertus, *cementarius*, was employed at St. Albans Abbey ; [3] of him it was said that in ' skill and labour he exceeded all masons of his time '. He was a man so well esteemed and of such importance that he was granted a house in the town. He was, of course, a layman.[4]

ii. Later the Abbot was not quite so successful in his choice, for in or about the year 1200 it is recorded that having assembled

> ' a number of chosen *cementarii* of whom, M. (*Master*) Hugh de Goldcliff was the chief, a deceitful but clever workman . . . it happened that by the design of the said Hugh, in addition to stealth, fraud and impertinence, and above all extravagance . . . that before the work had risen about the " loge ", the Abbot grew tired, weary and timid and the work languished . . .' later (and though not higher than the roof of the ' loge ') part of the walls fell with their own weight so that ' the wreck of images and flowers became a laughing stock of beholders. . . . The workmen therefore quitted in despair, nor did any wages reward their labours.' [5]

[1] There almost seems to have been one such when Richard Farleigh was engaged at Salisbury as master-mason, but this may be open to explanation.

[2] In a trenchant article on modern architects as compared to the early builders, a writer says that : ' at present (1872) there is no such thing as a building art. This is entirely lost. . . . No architect, as we understand the word, would have designed the Parthenon. . . . Ictinus, the so-called architect, was a cunning master-builder (σοφὸς οἰκοδόμος) the *working* head of a band of *working* men. The same is unquestionably true of Pheidias and his helpers. . . . So in our own old Churches and Cathedrals, the design was obviously done by the workman ; in fact there is no record of design at all. The work was " built ", or the stone was " cut " ; and that included what we call the design.' ' State of English Architecture,' *Quarterly Review*, April 1872, p. 295 et seq.

[3] Ferrey, ' Early Mediaeval Architects,' *R.I.B.A. Trans.*, 1865.

[4] The term *cementarius* infers a lay-man and the further references in the record clearly confirms it, and also that he lived out of the Convent.

[5] W. Papworth, op. cit. Surely no church would claim a scamp of this description—he must have been a lay-man !

This, though it is otherwise ill news, clearly shows that there was a ' master ' on whom the work depended. It also shows that there was a ' loge ', and workers—*chosen cementarii*—who were probably selected from a number of applicants ; and, lastly, that carved work —' flowers and images '—were already *in situ* though the record says the wall was not higher than the roof of the ' loge '. Of these matters later.

iii. In 1113, Arnold, a lay-brother[1] at Croyland Abbey, is reported as ' of the art of masonry a most scientific *master* '.

Facts are, however, badly against his scientific abilities, for the truth is that a good deal of this work at Croyland failed by virtue of bad foundations. It appears that these were laid on a peat soil ; they were of this ' scientific master's ' period. They consisted of large flat stones (each more than one man could carry) thrown apparently at random into the slough, and so left and so built upon !

iv. In 1179, after the disastrous fire at Canterbury Cathedral of 1174, the Chronicler says that :

' French and English workmen[2] were summoned, but they were of varying opinions, some asserting they could repair the columns without endangering the work above, others denying the possibility of this and saying that the whole church must be pulled down if the safety of the monks was to be ensured. And the possibility of these words being true filled them with grief, nor was it to be wondered at, for the monks could not hope that so large a work could be completed within their lifetime. But one, William of Sens, was present with the other workmen— a man both physically strong and a skilful worker in wood and stone,[3] and to him under the providence of God, the finishing of the work was committed, rather than to the others, on account of his experience and fame in such work. He proceeded to spend many days in careful investigations with the monks, both of the upper and lower walls, and the interior and exterior, so that the least damage might be sustained by the weaker portions. He went on preparing everything necessary for the work, either himself or deputing it to others, and when he saw that the monks were a little consoled he had to tell them that the pillars damaged by fire and the superstructure ought to be pulled down if they wished to have the work satisfactorily done. At last they were convinced and consented, which work he promised should be done, since they wanted to be secure.'[4]

[1] Actually recorded as a lay-man.

[2] Probably he means ' master-workmen ' in a consultative capacity ; this the sequence implies.

[3] ' *Vir* admodum strenuus, in ligno et lapide artifex subtilissimus.' Note *vir* : that word would not have been used of an obedientiary.

[4] Freely translated from the *Chron. Gervase of Canterbury*, Rolls Series, 1879, pp. 20 and 21.

Here then in the twelfth century is the evidence of the selecting of an accepted ' master ', a layman, to do the rebuilding work, and that the monks felt incapable of dealing with the matter at all. The ' master ' examines the buildings as they stand in ruin and danger : he advises : he prepares all the necessary materials : he sets the work in hand and for four years it progresses and reaches at length a considerable height, aided by at least one of the monks, if not more. The records then relate that an accident befalls the building, and the master, though injured and ill, still controls and directs : finally he has to give it up, but is allowed to advise the employment of another ' master '. The record continues : [1]

> ' When the triforia on each side and the upper windows were completed, and the machines [2] for turning the great vault ready, at the beginning of the fifth year, suddenly by the collapse of beams beneath his feet, he (the *artifex* [3]) fell to the ground amid a shower of falling masonry and timber from the height of the higher capital of the arch, perhaps fifty feet or more.
>
> Being badly injured by the fall, and bruised by stones and rubble, he was rendered helpless to go on with the work. No one else was in any way harmed. On the master craftsman alone fell the stern wrath of God—or the machinations of the devil.
>
> The master was badly injured, and though lying in bed with the ministrations of doctors to facilitate a speedy recovery, his hopes were shattered and his health did not improve. And so, as winter was setting in and the completion of the upper arch was urgently necessary, he entrusted this to a skilful and hard-working monk, then in charge of the masons. This procedure aroused much envy and strife among them—this man being, though young, held to be wiser than older and more influential men. But the master though still in bed gave directions as to what should be done first, and what next. . . . And finally since the master realized that by no doctor's skill and care could he be cured, he gave up the charge of the work and went back to his home in France. His successor was an Englishman, William by name, slight in physique but very skilful and ingenious in his work. He finished both transepts, the north and the south, in the summer of the fifth year, and made the ciborium which was fixed above the great altar and which had been ready for the year before, but had been unable to be finally fixed owing to the advent of the rainy season.' [4]

[1] ' After the departure of William of Sens the rebuilding went on under his successor, William the Englishman (1179–84) and the work becomes more distinctly insular in character.' Powell, *Mediaeval Architecture*, vol. i, p. 157.

[2] Centres.

[3] Here again the word used implies a lay-man, and that he was a worker.

[4] *Chron. of Gervase* in op. cit.

No doubt William of Sens, who was a Frenchman, brought French traditions with him and this his building strongly evidences —his colleague and successor, though an Englishman, can also be readily admitted as having been influenced thereby and he probably proceeded along the same lines—to this must be added the fact that large parts of the stonework were actually prepared in the Caen quarries (patterns being sent over) and, as custom was, practically finished there ready to be put into the building before it was sent to England.[1] This was quite a frequent practice to save weight in carriage from the quarry to the work.

v. At York, a document dated 1351, makes careful provision for William de Hoton—father of M. (Master) William de Hoton, mason. It gives him a dwelling and directs that he is to look after the work at the Cathedral, and he agrees that if certain contingencies arise such as his blindness or other calamitous disease, he will find an under-mason to go on with the work. His son was appointed later.

vi. In 1355 the Chapter of York issued certain ' orders for the masons and workmen '. The first and second masons who were called ' masters ' were to take an oath that they would cause ancient customs (set forth in the Order) to be observed—the hours of work-ing—the summons to work or to leave off, and many other regula-tions. All the men were certainly laymen brought to York for the purposes of buildings in hand.

vii. There is record in the fourteenth century of one ' Henry, surnamed Lathomus ' (from his trade) ; he was at Evesham and was largely employed on the work of the Abbey there ; probably he was responsible also for the beautiful chapel in St. Lawrence's Church near by.

viii. In the fourteenth century after the fall of the central tower at Ely the chronicler of the time said : [2]

> ' Our Sacrist, Alan (de Walsingham) was sore grieved . . . he spent great labour and much money in removing . . . the fallen stones and beams. Finally he measured out in eight divisions, *with the aid of an architect,*[3] the place where he thought to build the new tower ; and he set workmen to dig and search for the foundations of the eight stone columns . . . at last he began

[1] ' It was not French influence, but actually French work, pure and simple —that it was not taking root is at least suggested by a statement made by Mr. Papworth, that William the Englishman had something to do with the work in hand at Coventry in 1199, concerning which there has never been any claim of French feeling whatsoever.' *R.I.B.A. Proceedings,* 1861.

[2] *Historia Eliensis,* A.D. 1321.

[3] Here again the lay-mason is called in, but the monk only is named !

those . . . and the stonework they supported . . . at length with God's help the tower was brought to . . . consummation. . . .' It took twenty years in building.

Later, when Alan had been made Prior in 1341, there is a record which reads :

> Vos qui regnorum vidistis opus variorum,
> Hunc scitote Chorum pre cunctis esse decorum,
> Quem Frater Alanus fecit Constructor humanus
> Tunc Sacrista pius, nunc Prior egregius.' [1]

ix. Again in connexion with the tower and spire of Louth Church (fifteenth century) it is stated that one Lawrence, a mason, was paid 6s. 8d. for riding to his ' master ' [2] in the north country ' to speer him whether he would make an end of the *broach* (spire) and he said he would deal no more with it but he showed his counsel '. The account gives other statements of seeking the master for directions.[3]

x. Besides the aforementioned there were other and greater men ; such as William of Wykeham, Henry de Yevele (of Yeovil), John of Gloucester, John of Lincoln, John of Wheathampstead, Alcock of Worcester (and elsewhere), Sir Reginald Bray, and many more. All laymen at first, if not first and last !

These are a few of the instances in English records, and they clearly evidence the non-clerical worker.   But if the position be considered by analogy to known and better recorded instances in France [4] and elsewhere still further evidence may be noted, of which the following are examples.[5]

Early in the thirteenth century the Bishop of Amiens directed a certain layman, named in the chronicle as Master [6] Robert de Luzarches, to build the great cathedral of that city.   The record continues that he was succeeded in this work by Thomas and Regnault de Cormont—father and son—in the work as masters or architects.[7]   In witness of this an inscription in Old French existed in the nave of the cathedral, as follows :

[1] Cott. MS. Titus Ai.

[2] John Cole, who had previously been in charge at Louth, was the mason who designed the tower and spire.

[3] *Archaeologia*, vol. x, pp. 70-98, for very interesting accounts as to the sixteenth-century building expenses ; also Bond, *English Church Architecture.*

[4] *Dictionary of Architecture*, Audsley ; gives a long and interesting article.

[5] See *Mediaeval Art*, Lethaby, 1912, p. 243 et seq.   Here illustrations are also given.

[6] In the following instances of foreign record the term ' Master ' is almost invariably attached to the names given.

[7] ' The following of a master-mason by his sons is also to be noted at Strasburg where two of Erwin von Steinbach's sons continued the work he had commenced.' Prof. Simpson's *History of Architecture.*

In England there is the record at York in the succession of the Hotons, *c.* 1351.

CHIL · Q̄ · MAISTRE · YERT · DE · L'ŒUVRAIGE ·
MAISTRE · ROBERT · ESTOIT · NOMES ·
ET · DE · LUZARCHES · SURNOMES · [1]
MAISTRE · THOMAS · FU · APRES · LUY ·
DE · CORMONT · ET · APRES · SEN · FILZ ·
MAISTRE · REGNAULT · QUI · MESTRE ·
FIST · A · CHEST · POINT · CHI · CHESTE · LEITRE ·
QUE · L'INCARNACION · VALOIT ·
XIII · C · ANS · MOINS · XII · EN · FALOIT · [2]

Translation:

'. . . He who was master of the work, Master Robert was his name and de Luzarches was his surname. Master Thomas de Cormont was after him, and after him his son Master Regnault, who when master made this inscription to this point ; less than twelve years were wanting for the Year of our Lord to be 1300.' (i.e. 1288.)

La Sainte Chapelle in Paris has records of one Pierre de Montereau (or Montereu) who was a layman much esteemed in his day (the thirteenth century). He was also employed on other ecclesiastical work in the city, and was buried in the choir of Saint Germain des Prés, eighteen years after La Sainte Chapelle was completed. On the tomb he is named *Mestre Pierre de Montereul*,[3] and the design of that monument is said to have been based on that of ' Hugues Libergier, architecte de la célèbre église abbatiale de Saint-Nicaise (Rheims) mort en 1263 '.[4]

This man, Libergier, was buried in the Cathedral at Rheims. The tomb shows the figure of a young man in lay attire (gown, cloak, and cap) holding in his left hand the *virga geometralis*, or measuring rod, and in his right, a model of a church ; below on the right is a builder's square, and on the left a curiously shaped pair of compasses.[5]

---

[1] There is a street facing the south transept of Amiens Cathedral called *Rue Robert de Luzarches*, and at Rheims on the north side of the Cathedral *Rue Robert de Courcy*, evidently commemorating the master-masons of those names.　　　　　　　　　　　　　　　　　　[2] Audsley, op. cit.

[3] ' Doctor lathomorum ' is his designation on his tomb in St. Germain des Prés.　　　　[4] Guilhermey, *La Sainte Chapelle, Paris,* 1867.

[5] Didron, *Annales Archèologique*, vol. i, p. 145, records as follows :

' Libergier . . . il a les pieds sur des nuages et la tête en plein dans le ciel, où deux anges l'encensent comme s'il était un saint. Il tient à la main gauche le bâton de l'architecte, la verge géométrale (*virga geometralis*), si souvent nommée dans nos anciennes légendes, et dont l'architecte de Theodoris, roi des Visigoths, était déjà au VIe siecle. Cette règle est divisée en demi-traits au-dessous et au-dessus de la main, en traits pleins à l'endroit même où le main se pose. . . . Aux pieds de Libergier, à sa gauche, est la louve qui a monté les pierres de l'église ; à sa droite, l'équerre sous laquelle les assises se sont

On the lower part of the South Doorway at Notre Dame, Paris, is an inscription to the effect that in 1257, Master Jean, or John de Chelles was engaged on certain building work at that cathedral.[1]

Libergier's Tomb Slab.

alignées ; Libergier porte enfin de sa main droite, la main puissante le modèle idéal de l'église qu'il a bâtie ; il l'appuie contre sa poitrine comme son oeuvre chérie. . . . Libergier était laïque, ainsi que le prouve son costume purement civil. . . . La niche où Libergier se dresse est du XIIIe siecle. . . . Libergier fut donc trente-quatre ans à Saint Nicaise. Est-il mortjeune, comme on pourrait le croire à sa jeune et imberbe figure, d'après sa tombe.'

[1] ' Anno Domini MCCLVII mense februario idus secundo

Hoc fuit inceptum Christi genitricis honore,
Kallensi lathomo vivente Johanne magistro.'

Audsley, op. cit.

A like inscription is to be found over the Great Doorway at Strasbourg Cathedral.[1]

When Airard proposed a reconstruction of St. Remi in Rheims, eleventh century, ' he summoned men who were said to be skilled in architecture . . . he commenced to build.' ' *Quapropter viris*[2] *qui architecturae periti ferebantur ascitis . . . fabricam . . . erigere coepit.*' The same MS. later goes on to say: ' This building he almost destroyed, but left certain foundations, which the *architects* thought would be useful for the future buildings.' ' *Quo poene diruto et fundamentis quibusdam relictis, quae architectis*[3] *visa sunt necessaria fore futuris aedificiis, divinam domum coepit.*'

It is recorded in the *Chronicles of Bec*:

> ' Therefore when the foundations had been laid deep, the abbot himself surrounded by his monks laid the first stone of the foundations on the first day of Lent, and Ingelram, a builder of Notre Dame of Rouen, directed and aided in the construction. And to his superintendence the abbot entrusted the beginning and care of the work, and for the first year Ingelram worked hard at the building and constructed it with great success, altering the façade and increasing the length of the nave and wonderfully adorning it with two broad towers ; but after a year and a half he commenced to absent himself occasionally, neglecting the work and not finishing it as he had promised. When the abbot saw and understood this, he took wise council and when now a year and eight months had passed, he removed Ingelram from the sacred place and handed the work over to a master-builder, Walter of Melun, who finished it in the third year.' [4]

There are also some sculptured memorials to be found in continental buildings of certain master-masons. In the Duomo at Florence, a man bearing a baton (the *virga geometralis*) is shown directing two masons who stand on a scaffold and are setting blocks in what appears to be a tower.[5] At Semur is a figure of a layman bearing a square and a pair of compasses.[6]

At Stuttgart Spital Kirche is a corbel showing a mason with a roll and compasses.

[1] ' Anno Domini MCCLXXVII in die Beati Urbani hoc gloriosum opus incohavit Magister Ervinus de Steinbach.' Ibid.

[2] *Viris* = men, clearly laymen, in contra-distinction to monks or even lay-brethren. *Anselmi Itin.*, Leonis IX.

[3] An almost exceptional use of this term in early mediaeval records, though not bearing the modern meaning. It denotes, as in its Greek origin, the chief builder.   [4] *Opera Omnia Lanfranci*, 1648.

[5] Figured in Viollet le Duc's *Dictionnaire*, vol. i.

[6] Ibid.

A stall carving at Poitiers (thirteenth century) shows a man with a moulded tablet, a pair of dividers and other impedimenta.

In the glass of a chapel in Chartres Cathedral is another building scene, where are three masons and a hooded figure of an architect or master.[1]

Also, in a thirteenth-century window at Burgos Cathedral (Spain) are figures of masons at work.

There is not much of this sort of memorial to be found in English buildings ; but there is an inscription at Gloucester, concerning the central tower of the Cathedral, which records :

> ' Hoc quod digestum specularis opusque politum,
> Tullii haec ex onere Seabroke Abbate jubente.'

Abbot Seabroke, 1450–7, took down the tower as far as the Norman piers and proceeded to build the present beautiful upper work. He died before it was finished, and Robert Tully, a monk of the house, carried it on to completion.

The inscription is placed above the west window. Tully, who was evidently a man of parts, was afterwards made Bishop of St. Davids.

There was also a tomb-slab at Croyland Abbey, dated 1427, which showed a carved figure of William Warrington, master-mason there.[2]   And there are also two memorial stones in the abbey, one 1430, to a ' *Latomus in arte* ' and the other, 1490, to a ' *Latomus* '.

A mutilated figure in stone was discovered at Durham (*c*. 1820) holding in its hands a carved representation of a Church of contemporary period to its general work (early thirteenth century) and probably was the effigy of a master-mason.

Of sixteenth-century date there are two figures fixed against a house opposite Wooburn Church, Bucks.[3]   One of them has a compass and rule, and the other a quadrant and staff.[4]

There are some drawings in various manuscripts which supply further evidence.   One concerning St. Albans Abbey shows a workman or master receiving instructions from King Offa.[5]

These manuscript examples might be followed further.   They are

---

[1] Audsley, op. cit.

[2] Figured in the *Trans. of the Lodge Quatuor Coronati*, Condor, and also in Prior's *Gothic Art*, p. 385.   [3] See *Archaeologia*, xviii. 421.

[4] Over a window at Moreton Hall, Cheshire, is an inscription : ' Rychade Dale Carpeder made thies windows by the grace of God. MDLXI.'

[5] The master-mason has a square and an enormous pair of compasses. The masons are at work on the walls, and have a simple hoisting gear: Cott. MS., British Museum.   Also see the Plates and descriptive notes thereto, § 9, pp. 88–94.

interesting and instructive—see the Notes on Illustrations given in a later section.

Taken altogether these various evidences go to confirm the lay-master's position, and it seems admissible, therefore, to concur in general terms with Mr. Papworth's statement when he says:

> ' My opinion is that it is to the master-mason as a general rule we may turn for the actual designs of all the well-known erections of the Middle Ages.' [1]

Warrington's Tomb Slab.[2]

and when he further adds, some years later and after much further research:

> ' these master-masons were generally the architects during the Mediaeval period in England. The " master of the works " may have been so and probably the " clerk of the works " was so in the latest times.' [3]

---

[1] *R.I.B.A. Trans.*, 1861.

[2] From Prior's *Gothic Art*, by permission of the publishers, Messrs. Bell & Co.

[3] W. Papworth, *R.I.B.A. Trans.*, 1887.

The Audsley brothers confirm this opinion and say:

> ' In the documents preserved to us which relate to English
> buildings, the almost exclusive use of the term mason (*cemen-*
> *tarius*) goes far to prove that here (in England) at least, the
> architect and the master-mason were in many instances one
> and the same person.' [1]

And Mr. Kingley Porter, in a recent work embodying much
research says: [2]

> ' For the thirteenth century . . . the Abbot or Bishop or
> Chapter entrusted to a lay architect or master-builder the
> drawing of the plans and the supervision of the work. . . . Some
> archaeologists . . . believe that in the first half of the twelfth
> century things were otherwise. At this period monasticism
> dominated architecture, and it has been generally inferred that
> the monks themselves were the master-builders and even the
> masons . . . yet . . . at most this is no more than a plausible
> conjecture.
>
> The silence of the chroniclers is exasperating. Over and
> over again all that is stated is that the abbot began to build
> . . . or such and such work was consecrated. In the thirteenth
> century the word " build " must be understood to mean
> " caused to be built ".'

As to the custom in France, one writer says:

> ' The master of the work generally lived at the foot of the
> cathedral, where, under heavy awnings of grey canvas, he had
> established his workshop, his " lodge " (*loge*), to use the
> expression of the time. It was a little city of workmen
> governed by the architect, paid and supported according to
> accounts kept by the clerks of the church. There lived, under
> a common authority, the various artisans of the work, from
> the masons and carpenters to plumbers and workers in stained
> glass. They laboured in closed workshops, heated in winter.' [3]

These master-masons, as their order of ' master ' implied, were
accredited members of mason guilds and were not in any respect
of the Church. That they were free and travelled about the country
at will cannot be gainsaid, and the probability was that they drew
after them part or perhaps the whole of the guild with which they
were connected and to which their names added lustre.

§ 3. On Contracts in Building

So far as actual records of building contracts go there are comparatively few, but in what there are the case is very clearly stated
and shows that master-masons, carpenters, and others actually

[1] Audsley, *Dictionary of Architecture.*   [2] *Mediaeval Architecture*, 1922.
[3] *Middle Ages*, Fr. Brentano, op. cit., p. 225.

entered into agreements from time to time, and bound themselves to do certain works and occasionally even to find the appurtenant labours in other trades than their own as required for the completion of the general works under contract, and also to supply the necessary materials, plant, &c., throughout ; at other times these things were found for them.

The period over which records of these contracting masters are to be found is a very wide one, beginning in the fourteenth century [1] or even earlier.

Amongst these agreements there is a London contract wherein one Simon de Canterbury agreed in 1308 [2] to build a house, described in detail in the document, for William de Haningtone for the sum of £9 5s. 4d. and a parcel of ' half-a-hundred ' martin skins and fur for a robe, for Haningtone was a pelterer [3] and here paid partly in kind. Simon was to complete the work ' down to the locks '.

Another contract,[4] dated in 1314 on Monday after the Feast of St. Martin, was for a house at Lapworth in Warwickshire; under its clauses ' *Will' Heose, masoune*, and *Joh'n de Pesham de Roventon* ' agreed with Sir John de Byssopesdon, for the building of a house of ' *pere fraunche bone convenable e byen overe* '. It goes on to give many details of the structure, size of rooms and so forth, and that Sir John is to find ' *merym* ' [5] *charpentie, sabeloun*,[6] *chaus* [7] '. The price to be paid was agreed at ' *Vynt e sing mars* ' (xxv marks).

At Lincoln there is an enrolment of an agreement,[8] dated in 1316, between Sir John de Sandale, clerk, and Master Roger de Laghton, ' carpenter,' witnessing that Roger has agreed to build two ranges [9] (*rengees*) of Sir John's houses in Boston, whereof the one on the north side shall be 136 feet in length measured by the king's ell (*de laune*) and 16 feet in breath, and the other, on the south side, shall be 185 feet in length and 15 feet in breadth, for which Roger shall find the beams (*maerem*'), the great posts which are to be

---

[1] In French records there is a contract, dated in 1261 made between Martin de Lonay and the Abbot of St. Giles in Languedoc, for the completion of the abbey church there ; it provides that Martin is to receive ' 100 pounds of Tours ' and he is to have two sous for each working day ; he is further to have right to take his meals at the Abbot's table except on feast-days, and is to have a horse. Brentano, op. cit., p. 226.

[2] London Letter Book, fol. xcvi ; also Riley, *Mems. of London.*

[3] A fur or skin dealer.

[4] Given *in extenso* in Hudson Turner's *Domestic Architecture*, vol. ii, p. 5.

[5] *Meremium* = timber for carpenters.

[6] Sand.   [7] Lime.

[8] Cal. Close Rolls, 9 Edward II.   [9] Corridors or galleries (?).

14 feet in height (*en estaunce*) and 1 foot in breadth, and all the other timber and things for the carpentry, so that the two ranges shall be well and properly built and fitted (*apparailles*) with gardrobes and all other things pertaining to carpentry by Whitsuntide then next following. For this work Sir John agreed to pay Master Roger £37 ; to be paid, £10 at the Purification, £10 at Easter, and the balance so soon as the work was done.

Witnesses : John de la Gutre, Geoffrey de Sutton, and Roger de Sutton of Boston; Stephen the clerk. Dated at Netelham, 30 January, 9 Edward II.

> *Memorandum : that Roger came into chancery at Netelham, on the aforesaid day, and acknowledged the above deed.*

Under the date July 1334, Richard Farleigh agreed with the Chapter of Salisbury Cathedral ' to superintend, direct and appoint useful and faithful masons and plaisterers ' (*cementarii*, probably mistranslated) for the work of the tower of the Cathedral.[1] There was, however, a regular *master of works* employed on the fabric, which rather suggests that Farleigh acted more in the capacity of architect despite the fact of his contract to find and direct men. Later, 1394, the Chapter entered into an agreement with Nicholas Portland for certain works to the spire,[2] and not long thereafter Elias de Derham was appointed superintendent and held office for twenty years.[3]

In 1395 two masons, Richard Washbourn and John Swalwe, entered into a contract with Richard II for work in ' la Grande Sale deinz le Paloys de Westmonstier '. The indenture [4] defines the stone to be used, its sizes and the progress of the work, and to whose design and approval it is to be carried out, namely, that of ' Mestre Henri Zeueley (Yevele) '. There are also other contracts concerning Westminster Hall.

In the same year this master—Henry Yevele—and another mason, Stephen Lote, signed an indenture with the king for making of ' une toumbe de fyne Marbre ' for the late Queen.[5] It is to be noted that in the former case Yevele designs and approves—in the latter he contracts.

---

[1] Dodsworth, *Salisbury Cathedral*, p. 151 ; also W. Papworth, *R.I.B.A. Trans.*, 1887, p. 210. Farleigh very probably did the central tower at Pershore, Worcs., at a later period ; the similarity between it and Salisbury is otherwise quite inexplicable.

[2] Ibid., p. 158.

[3] Ibid., quoting Leland's *Itinerary*, vol. iii.

[4] Rymer, *Feodera*, tom. vii, p. 794.   [5] Rymer, op. cit.

By a contract dated 1412, commencing—' Ende' tur' ecclesii de Cataik' [1]—between Dame Katerine of Burgh, William of Burgh and Richarde of Cracall, mason, the latter agreed ' to make the Kirke of Keterick newe als Werkmanschippe and mason crafte will . . . to fynde alle the laboreres and servys ptenand (service pertaining) . . . sall take downe and ridde of the stane werke (i. e. of the old church) . . . carry and bere all the stanewarke of the alde Kirke to the place whare the newe Kirke sall be made. . . .' The contract goes on to describe the work, gives dimensions of the parts of the buildings, heights of walls, particulars of the windows, arches, buttresses, &c., &c., and states the date of completion when Richarde is to have ' tenne markes of monie and a gown of William wering to his reward . . . if the Kirke be endid at the terme. . . .'

There is the contract for the Great Bell-Tower of Bury St. Edmunds,[2] dated 1425.

> ' This bille indentyd maad att Bury the xxv day of Auguste, ye the yer of Kyng Herry the vj . . . betwen Willyam Abbot . . . P'our & Couent . . . and John Wode, masoun of Colchestř . . . the seyd John Wode schal werke wᵗ on švāt vp on the stepil in all mañ thynges that longe to fremasounrye . . . for hys stypend and hys šuantes x*li*. yn mony at iiij termys in the yeer . . . be the handys of the maysť of the werkes assynyd be the Chapetr . . . schal haue hys bord in the Couentys halle for hym and hys man, for hym self as a gentilman, and for hys švaunt as for a yoman ; And therto too robys, on for hym self of gentilmannys liuere, and for hys švaunt anothir of yeomānys lyvere . . . (or in lieu thereof) xxiijs. iiij*d*. . . . In Wytnesse . . .' (&c., &c.).

This Covenant was for a period of seven years. But by a later agreement the abbot was to be at liberty to send as many workmen to the building as he thought well, giving Wode, as master of the works, for wages and maintenance 3s. per man per week in winter and 3s. 4d. in summer.[3]

By another and very much later Deed the abbot of Bury St. Edmunds engaged John Arnold and Herman Remond, brick-burners, to make as many bricks in a year as they were able for the manor-house at Chevington ;[4] the abbot finding the materials and a chamber and paying 2s. per thousand, and also allowing them a cloak and hood each.[5]

---

[1] Rainè, *Catterick Church*, Yorks. 'Indenture for the tower of the Church at Catterick.'   [2] *Archaeologia*, vol. xxiii, p. 330.

[3] Winter wages, from Michaelmas to Ladyday, were always less on account of the shorter hours of daylight.

[4] Dugdale, *Monasticon*.   [5] *Archaeologia*, vol. xxiii, p. 332.

Lengthy contracts, dated in 1440, for work at Eton College are worth careful note.[1] Also that for the general building work for the Chapel at King's College, Cambridge, an undertaking which was set in hand under the directions in the will of Henry VI; the contract is dated in 1447.[2] A further and quite as interesting contract was made at a later date for the vault-work, in which minute details were set forth (4 Hen. VIII).[3]

An indenture for the erection of a house in High Street, Bristol, is preserved:[4] it was dated 1472, and agreed as follows:

> 'This indenture made between Alice Chester of Bristol, widow, sometime the wife of Harry Chester of Bristol, draper, on the one party, and Stephen Morgan of Bristol, carpenter, on the other party, Witnesses, that the said Stephen hath covenanted with the same Alice and him bindeth by these presents to make well, workmanly, and surely of good timber

[1] See Britton, *Architectural Antiquities*. Willis & Clarke edit. vol. i.

[2] Ibid., vol. ii. It provides that . . . the Church of the said College . . . 'shall containe 288 feete of assise (statutable feet) in *length*, without any yles, and all of the *wideness* of 40 feete, . . . the *walls* of the same church to be in height 90 feete, imbattled, vawted and chare roffed, sufficiently boteraced . . . in the east end . . . a windowe of xj dayes . . .' (the Will further particularises other details and, later, other collegiate buildings). Then it goes on to specify wages, &c., '. . . the *master* of the workes, 50 *lib.*, for the *clerk* of the workes 13 *lib.* 6s. 8d., for the *chiefe mason*, 16 *lib.* 13s. 4d., for the *chiefe carpenter* 12 *lib.* 8s., for the *chiefe smith* 6 *lib.* 13s. 4d. and for the purveyors, either of them a 6d. the day. . . .' Provisions for the finding of monies follow. See also Nichol's *Collection of Royal Wills*, 1780.

[3] This document is also of some length. It commences with the agreement of certain College Officials with 'the advise and agrement of Mr. *Thomas Larke* Surveyur of the King's workes there' of the one part, and '*John Wastell* master mason of the said works, and *Herry Semerk* (or Severick) oon of the wardens of the same on the other partye, witnesseth . . . that the said John Wastell and Herry Semerk shall make and sett up . . . a good, suer and sufficient *Vawte* . . . workmanly wrought, made and sett up after the best handlinge and forme of good workmanship, according to a *Platt* thereof made and signed. . . . And the seid John Wastell and Herry Semerk shall provide and fynde . . . ston of *Weldon quarryes* as shall suffise . . . together with lyme, sand, scaffoldyng, cinctures, molds, ordinances and every other thyng . . . as well workmen and laborers, as all manner of stuff and ordinannces that shall be required . . .'; The contractors are to have the scaffold of two 'severeyes' for themselves in recompense for 'the great cost . . . remevyng the grate scaffold'. The Contractors also are granted the use of 'gynnes, wheles, cables, robynatts, sawes', &c., but these are to be returned to the Provost of the College on the completion of the works. 'They shall performe and clerely fynysh all the said vawte within the terme and space of three yeres'; and are to be paid £1,200 or £100 for each severy of the vault. Ibid.

[4] *The Livery Companies*, Hazlitt, p. 406.

and boards a new House in the High Street of Bristol, with floors, windows, doors, and partitions and all other things of timber work belonging to the same house except laths and lattices, which said new house shall be set between the tenement called the Bull on the one party, and the tenement in which one John, a Corviser,[1] now dwelleth in, on the other party, containing in length 19 feet and 5 inches of size and in wideness 10 feet and 4 inches; and the said Stephen shall make in the said shop, a hall above the same with an oriel, a chamber above the hall with an oriel and another chamber above that by the feast of the Annunciation of our Lady next coming for which house so to be made by the same Stephen the said Alice granteth and her bindeth by this present to payments the said Stephen 6l. 18s. 4d. sterling, that is to say at the feast of the Nativity of our Lord next coming 3l., at the flooring of the said house 38s. 4d. and at the end of the same work 40s. Also it is accorded that it shall be lawful to the same Stephen to have and to take as his own all the old timber of the said old house without any gainsaying of the same Alice or any other for her or in her name. In witness thereof the parties aforesaid to these indentures interchangeably have set their seals. Given the 17th day of the month of November, in the 12th year of the reign of King Edward the fourth.'

The contract, already referred to, for building the tower and spire (*broach*) at Louth, in 1501, brings these relationships up into the sixteenth century, when building by contract was becoming the usual method of procedure, and there are many instances to be found.

Occasionally contract work was carried out by other tradesmen than masons and carpenters, such as for the plumbers' work, in 1367 and 1370, given in the York Fabric Rolls.[2] There is also a plastering contract of the fourteenth century, as follows: dated in 1317 it was a somewhat unusual agreement and was made between a master-plasterer, Adam le Plastrer, citizen of London and the Earl of Richmond, by which the former agreed to 'find plaster of Paris, at my own proper charges, good and sufficient, without default . . . plaster and complete the hall . . . well and befittingly within and without, also the tewells [3] to the summit . . . for xxiv*l* sterling . . . which the said earl has paid me beforehand . . .' [4]

---

[1] Cordwainer or shoemaker.

[2] *York Fabric Rolls*, op. cit., pp. 179 and 182.

    1367. Indenture with John, the plumber. ' Johannes Plomer, de Blayke stret ' a contract for his work ' suis manibus, et non per substitam personam ', and later another in

    1370. Indenture with ' Johannem filium Adae le Plummer de Beverlaco ', to serve the Chapter in his trade. See later, p. 59.

[3] Flues or louvres.

[4] An extraordinary contract where work is paid for prior to its execution.

A few other instances of contracted work are:

1382.   By an indenture Nicholas Typerton agreed to build an aisle to St. Dunstan's Church, Thames Street, London ' selòn la devyse Mestre Henry Iveleghe '.[1] Here appears some suggestion of the architect-overseer, one to whose directions work is to be done by a contractor.

1398.   John de Middleton entered into a contract at Durham for the conventual dormitory.

1401.   Robert Daynwell and William Landes, masons, signed a contract, undertaking to complete the above work. In the contract ' scaffoldes, seyntrees, and flekes ' are mentioned as necessary.

1412.   Richard de Cracall, mason, contracted to rebuild Catterick Church, Yorks., in three years.

1421–2. Three masons, Thomas Ampleforde, John Garett, and Robert Mannsell contracted to build a bridge at Catterick.

1426.   Walberswick steeple in Suffolk was contracted for by two masons, Richard Rupel of Dunwich and Adam Powle of Blythburg.

1435.   William Horwod ' freemason ' contracted to build Fotheringhay Church. There is evidence of some sort of overcontrol, for the agreement says the work is to be done ' by oversight of maisters of the same craft '. A ' clerke of the werke ' is also mentioned, and Horwod agrees to ' yeilde his body to prison ' if he fails to get the work done as set forth in the indenture.

1475–80. A considerable portion of Magdalen College, Oxford, was built under a contract with one William Orcheyerd, mastermason.

1476.   John Wolrich, master-mason, contracted for and did work at King's College, Cambridge.

1542.   Covenant to build a Cross in Coventry, in place of one then standing in Cross Cheping. It was agreed to be ' in form, fashion, and due proportion in all points of a Cross . . . in the town of Abingdon in the County of Berks.'

§ 4. ON GUILDS GENERALLY

In considering the guild question, careful discrimination is necessary to avoid confusion of those of mason-craft with the manufacturing or trade-guilds of the cities and towns. Of the latter there was one for nearly every trade in all the towns in the kingdom, with their rules of entry, of training, of mastership, and general trade regulations, &c.[2] Each *mistery*, as the trade was

---

[1] Harl. Charter, Brit. Mus. This refers to Henry Yevele better known in connexion with his work at Westminster Abbey and the Guildhall, London. See Master-masons, p. 52, and *supra* p. 30.

[2] Seven years' service was required except for sons of masters, and no master could have more than one apprentice. After the apprenticeship period

termed, was jealously guarded alike from invasion from without [1] and corruption from within. The mason-guilds had a great deal in common with all trade-guilds, but they were controlled by some quite special and exceptional orders, as indeed the nature of their work and the varying places of its execution demanded. They were not tied to particular places as were the other guilds and, although some have even argued that the term ' freemason ' evidences this freedom to move, it is entirely doubtful if such be its whole significance.

Freemasons of to-day advance a claim of origin with the craft-masons of a very remote past, but their case is by no means proved yet. Indeed, the general craft idea is quite different nowadays from what it was in the actual building period : then the guilds were distinctly commercial institutions, and their affairs and principles of business concern, but to-day the purpose and atmosphere has so far changed as to have almost entirely lost likeness, and such like-ness as may be noted still lies only in qualities of moral and social fellowship—all business and commercial purposes, all the labours of the lodge and the transmission of the trading concerns of the ' mistery ' having entirely disappeared.

Leaving earliest periods out of the present quest—it may be briefly stated that it is averred that in Rome a *Collegium* of Artificers existed ; that after the fall of the city they (or their descendants) are believed to have settled in the Como district ; that they spread their influence thence all over Western Europe, and finally, that they merged with the mason-craft guilds of the Middle Ages ; how much farther than this they may be followed is a wholly debatable proposition.

' In England they (the Guilds) were existent and powerful in Anglo-Saxon times: the laws of Alfred the Great refer to them and so do the Ordinances of Edgar ; and in their own laws and orders the early and later guilds alike had most salutary requirements and conditions both as to the personal conduct

was concluded then service had to be rendered as a journey-man and finally the candidate qualified for mastership.

[1] For instance, in London, after the Great Fire, 1666, there was a move made by the freemen against foreign labour in the various branches of the building trade which had then been specially admitted by an Act of Parliament. The Carpenters', Masons', Bricklayers', and other Companies petitioned the Court of Aldermen, setting forth the ancient practices and usages and complaining of the violation thereof by the ' foreigners '. Eventually they succeeded in ousting them, and many hundreds were out of employment. (*Foreigners* does not here mean those from beyond the seas but any who were not freemen of the City of London.) *Great Fire of London*, Bell.

of their members within the body politic and the general community in whose midst they lived and whose interest they were bound by oath to conserve.'[1]

Professor Merzario—(an able Italian antiquary) who has made very exhaustive searches into the continental relationship of the guild question—says that the Comacine influence spread and dominated art 'in Germany, Gaul, and elsewhere'.[2] To this averment Professor Camille Poito, another learned inquirer, has added:

> ' Some have wished to demonstrate a secret Society having the monopoly of the architectural arts . . . while others have wished to make them out ignorant masons. . . . It is certain that . . . Como . . . wise and beautiful in its own time, from which art was born, after a series of transformations, the pointed arch styles, found so much favour in Germany, France, and England . . . was able to become perhaps the base of the Italian art . . .[3]

In the English mediaeval period very definite evidence of the acknowledgement of the rules of guild relationships is to be found in the York Fabric Roll records. Indeed, not only an acknowledgement, but a demand by the Chapter that such regulations should be fully observed.[4] A definite annual pledge-day was appointed, and in the Roll of 1371 the occasion is set forth when the workmen came before it and swore to accept the ordinations of the Chapter as to their working hours and other regulations.[5]

A fifteenth-century manuscript charter in the British Museum, referring to the masons of York, says: ' that congregations of masons were to be held annually or triennially for the examination of master-masons respecting their knowledge of the craft '.[6]

It is not, however, within the province of this inquiry to discuss further the interminable question of guild origins and their affairs or

---

[1] Lambert, *Two Thousand Years of Gild Life.*

[2] Merzario, *Maestri Comacini*, vol. i, p. 98.

[3] Ravenscroft, in *Further Notes on the Comacine Masters*, quotes this and much else in attempting to prove the Comacine influence on art and the long descent of masonic traditions.

[4] *Curialitates* : Et dati cementariis in le pleghdai de curialitate, ex consuetudine, 20s. Dati vj carpintariis in eodem die, de curialitate, 2s. In potu dato super singulis solucionibus in uno . . . 13s. In potu dato communibus operariis in fabrica et apud Usee, per annum, 35s. 6d. Summa 70s. 6d. York. *Compotus Roll*, anno MCCCLXXI, Surtees Soc., op. cit., p. 11.

[5] *Ordinacio Cementariorum*, 1370. *Fabric Rolls*, Surtees Soc., op. 181–2. A document of greatest interest. There was a very similar order made some twenty years earlier. Vide Harl. MS. 6971.

[6] Condor, *Hole Craft*. This and other references already given goes to show the coherency of affairs under which architecture developed.

even of mason-guilds as historic institutions. It must suffice to recognize them as existent in the mediaeval period and as including in their fellowship the masters of building and of the crafts related thereto.[1] These guilds indubitably had a dominant bearing on architectural development throughout the ages.

Let it be also said that in the truest days of the guilds their aims and purposes were based on the very highest of ideals: to serve with simple truth ; to do well; to charge fairly; to avoid usury, and to deal honourably alike as between worker and worker and with the community. The spirit of the guild as a whole was its sense of responsibility for the trade, hence, guild service at its best became a sure guarantee of value and fitness, and it ensured the proper training of the workman. All unscrupulous bargainings, all fore-stalling of materials or markets, and all self-seeking and unfair advantages were alike abhorrent to its creed. If there were any good bargains to be made, then they must be shared with the trade. These principles were fundamental in the guilds of all trades in their purest periods, and the social and religious aspect of all their relationships were always kept in memory and observance.

But in their decay, in the obtrusion of the self-seeker—when the organizations degenerated, to be mere centres of conspiracy for the purpose of raising prices and ' cutting the market '—in a word, unions of workers minded only to exploit the community for selfish advance—then the evil of their existence had to be recognized and the institutions suppressed.[2] This at first was by watchfulness and by minor State regulations, but, finally, by enactments to obliterate the guilds and to forbid the gathering of their congregations—and thereafter they ceased to be.

In 3 Henry VI, the ' yearly congregations and confederies ' having become so markedly evil and exercising so debasing an effect on the operative handicrafts, an Act was passed to forbid their meetings on pain on conviction of punishment for felony. It is probable that though the masons' guilds, in common with others throughout the kingdom, had seriously overstepped constitutional limits, this Act was found to be too stringent, and it was, therefore, repealed by 2 and 3 Edward VI, which permitted *freemasons* to follow their craft

---

[1] Notes on the London Livery Companies as to building trades, see Appendix II, p. 95. The London Mason Guild is referred to in various enactments *temp*. Ed. III and thereafter.

[2] See further, Wyclif's *Grete Curs*, op. cit : ' . . . men of sutel craft, as fre masons and othere . . . non of hem schal do ought but only hewe stone, though he myght profit his maistir twenti pound bi o daies werk bi leggyng on a wal, withouten harm or penyng himself. See hou this wickid peple conspireth. . . .'

in any town, whether 'free' of it or not, always providing they were 'free' of some given town or city.[1]

§ 5. ON GUILD LODGES

Here the masonic principle evidences itself again and with additional emphasis. Lodges there were—but the curious factor about the mason lodges was in the mobility that they had. There were probably such lodges or guild houses in many of the larger towns, and these were quite apart from those of ordinary trade guilds, and there were also certain Great Guilds. If that of St. Mary's at Lincoln[2] was in fact a mason-guild of this sort it was a very notable instance; the building it occupied still exists. Other and lesser lodges are to be noted by mention in records of their construction, appointments, or contents. For instance : the reference (*supra*) of the Abbot of St. Albans to the arrested progress of the front wall when 'not higher than the roof of the *loge*'—or in the records at York in 1355, and again in 1399, when an inventory of the tools in the *loge* or masons' workshop is given.[3]

Records also at various places refer to the provision, the extension, or the repair of *loges*.[4] These localized lodges were usually timber-built, they are known to have existed at St. Albans, Canterbury, York, Durham, Wells, and elsewhere.[5] They also provided the

[1] Cunningham, Paper to International Hist. Congress, 1913, *Notes on the Originations of the Mason-Craft in England*, British Academy, vol. for 1913.

[2] Referred to in some records on the *Great Guild*. See W. Watkins, *R.I.B.A. Journal*, 1913, p. 157, and 1914, p. 282, where he avers it was a mason guild and the most important one in the country. See below.

[3] The York references are most interesting ; the first concerns the *Ordinances for the Masons* under date 1370. ' Itte es ordayned by ye Chapitre of ye kirk of Saint Petyr of York, yat all ye Masonns y^t sall wyrke . . . in ye loge in ye close bysyde ye forsayde kirk als arly als yai may see skilfully by daylighte . . . sall stande yar trewly wyrkande atte yair werke all ye day . . . yf yt be alle werkday . . . till itte be hegh none, smytyn by ye clocke . . .' The *loge* is further mentioned as where they are to 'stande yare trewely ande bysily wyrkande'. The hours of work, summer and winter, are given, and provision made for sundry defaults. There is reference also to the 'Maistyr Masoun' and to 'ye Mayster & ye Kepers of ye werke '. See *Fabric Rolls*, op. cit., p. 181. Note as to the second reference is given later, see 'Tools, &c.', § 7, and pp. 17–18, *Fabric Rolls*, op. cit.

[4] At Windsor Castle it is recorded, sixteenth century, that the 'old lodge' used by the masons had to be cleared away 'wyche Lodge ffyll downe by Reson of Wynde '. Hope, *Windsor Castle*, p. 248. References occur over and over again concerning these structures.

[5] Watkins, op. cit., and others. See also *Vale Royal Ledger-book*, Lancs. and Cheshire Record Society, for the building *c.* 1278 of the lodge and dwellings for the masons there as among the preliminaries to the building operation.

workshop (*laborarium* or *apertorium*) for the more open affairs of the lodge.[1] Lodges of this sort were necessary for carrying-on the mason works of any large building enterprise. In connexion with the larger ones or on the more important works they doubtless also included a school for the training of apprentices. If very extensive works were in hand probably a more permanent structure was set up, and such as these may have become centres of mason resort—Grand Lodges—whereto annual assemblies could be summoned.

On the other hand, these places of assembly may have been quite independent guild houses. Such must have existed in various towns in England. In London, for example, there were annual fore-gatherings óf the craft, and there is abundant evidence of these meetings—though not of where they were held, but they can scarcely have been held in the lodge of any particular work in progress.

Mr. W. Watkins, in the papers already referred to, gives it as his considered opinion that from these conclaves the progressive stages of architectural development were issued, and this may have some truth ; but when he goes on to suggest that there was but one Great Guild or Grand Lodge in the kingdom, namely, at Lincoln, and that its guild house was that known as St. Mary's Guild House in that city, then it is impossible to agree with him.[2] That, from the conferences of the masters and the agreements to which they came in their meetings, the explanation is to be found of the general conformity of design throughout the land is probably correct. But it is quite another thing to say that all of it—everything—is to be referred to Lincoln.[3] Doubtless a good deal may be attributed to

---

[1] Leader Scott, *Cathedral Builders*, p. 207. The lodge usually consisted of two apartments—one being reserved for greater privacy of conclave or work; this was also the custom on the Continent. ' The most important room (*chambre aux traits*) in which the master drew his plans and made light wooden models of the various parts of the building. These plans or models were known as the " malles ".' Fr. Brentano, op. cit., p. 225. See also p. 28, *supra*.

[2] ' There is much to show that local guilds of masons were not under any central masonic origin such as was suggested by Leader Scott.' Prior, *Basis of Gothic Architecture*, a paper read before the Architectural Association, Feb. 1901.

[3] Mr. Watkins says in the *R.I.B.A. Journal* : ' I am emboldened to sug-gest that Lincoln was the place, and St. Mary's Guild the building, in which the arts and crafts were taught for several centuries.' (Jan. 1913).
' I repeat the suggestion that the head-quarters of our English mediaeval building fraternity were established in this Guild building at Lincoln.' (Feb. 1914.)
But despite these daring averments, be it noted that when the guilds were suppressed and the property of St. Mary's ' given ' to the city of Lincoln in 1548, it was ' with the consent of the fraternity, brethren and *sisters* ', and

Lincoln, particularly in the thirteenth century, but without question there were other dominant centres. It is too much to suppose that all the masters of the kingdom came to Lincoln or that St. Mary's at its largest could have contained them if they did.

There were very definite laws and orders for the conduct of these lodges both as to the behaviour of the members and as to the treatment of works: for example, at York there is a record: [1]

> ' In 1370 Robert of Patrington and 12 other masons came before the Chapter and swore to observe the rules. Among them (the rules) that no mason shall be received at work . . . but he is first proved a week or more . . . if found sufficient . . . to be received with the assent of the master and the keepers of the work and of the master mason and sware upon the book that he shall truly and busily at his power, without any manner of guiles, feints, or deceits keep whole all the points of the . . . ordinance . . . ' &c.

A quaint poem in fifteenth-century manuscript gives the orders of the masonic rule.[2] It consists of a series of fifteen Articles each dealing with various aspects of craft-rule.

> *Hic incipit articulus primus.*
>
> .   .   .   .   .   .
> The mayster mason moste be ful securly
> Bothe stedefast, trusty and trewe.
>
> .   .   .   .
> And paye thy fellows after the coste
> As vytaylys goth thenne, wel thou woste ;
> And pay them trewly, apon thy fay,
> What that they deserven may ;
> .   .   .   .   .   .   (and so on).

The second article declares:

> That every mayster that ys a mason
> Most ben at the generale congregacyon
> (&c., &c.)

The third says, that apprenticeship shall be for seven years ; and later articles, that apprentices shall not be charged for as if journeymen ; that ' no mayster schal supplante other ', and that none shall ' deprave his fellow's work ', and finally the fifteenth article requires heedfulness by the master—' lest hyt wolde turne the crafte to schame a(nd) hymself to mechul blame '.

There also followed other points of ordination, amongst which—

this last mentioned section of the body politic of the guild that then owned and gave the building is surely a complete argument against its then being a mason-guild of any sort, whatever it may have been at other times.

[1] *York Fabric Rolls.*
[2] See J. O. Halliwell, *Early History of Freemasonry.*

that nothing that transpired in the 'logge' should be told—'Kepe hyt wel to gret honowre'[1]—that various moral faults in life be avoided and that those who lived evilly, 'unbuxom' members, were to be expelled at the annual assemblies. Even powers of imprisonment of contrariants are stated.

Another record says:[2]

> 'noe mason make moulds nor noe square nor no rule to any rough lyers within the Lodge nor without to hew nor mould stones with noe mould of his own making.'

and yet another in the seventeenth century:[3]

> 'you shall not make any mould, square or rule to mould stone withal but such as is allowed by the fraternity.'

All this goes to show the exclusiveness of the craft and the difficulty—the impossibility—of any outside person, whether of the Church or the laity, obtaining entry to the fellowship of the craft or knowledge of its procedures. It evidences very definitely the sort of person the mediaeval builder must have been and the means by which he learned how to deal with the building matters entrusted to his care. He must have been a guildsman holding under oath the secrets and qualifications of his craft, otherwise he could neither claim authority over the workers nor knowledge in the methods of procedure ; he must also have been a loyal attendant of one of the periodical congregations of masters—at a Grand Guild, such as St. Mary's at Lincoln (if it were such), whereat the progress of design and the influences controlling it were discussed and future treatments determined upon. Definite information of any direct sort will probably never be forthcoming. The conclaves were private and the traditions handed on by oral communications only, and there are now only left to us the 'sermons in stone' to inform as to what must have been said and done.

Notes on the interesting matter of *Masons' marks*, which are to be found so frequently in old work, would be interesting, but the subject is too special for discussion here. References to these marks may be found in Gould's *Freemasonry*, already mentioned.[4]

---

[1] Secrecy as to its affairs was as carefully observed then as in any modern masonic lodge.
> 'The prevystye of the chamber telle he no mon,
> Ny yn the loggs whatsyever they done.' *Articles.*
To keep the door the Exeter Rolls state: 1405 'one runnyng bar for the door of the logge, 5d.' Oliver, *Hist. of Exeter.*

[2] *York Fabric Rolls*, sixteenth century.   [3] Ibid.

[4] See also *Journal Archaeol. Assoc.*, 1847 and 1850 ; *Associated Reports*, 1861 ; *R.I.B.A. Trans.*, 1844–9 and 1868–9 ; *The Builder*, vols. i, vi, vii, xiii, and xviii ; and *Archaeologia*, vol. xxx.

Worcestershire masons' marks are dealt with in a valuable paper in the *Associated Reports* which was read before the Worcester Archaeological Society a few years ago.

The nomenclature and development of mouldings is another branch of mediaeval building research of very considerable interest; the former was dealt with by the Rev. Robert Willis in a communication to the Cambridge Antiquarian Society [1] which has been already referred to, but nothing much appears to have been done with the latter since F. A. Paley's small book on *Gothic Mouldings* was published in 1877, and Edward Sharpe's greater work issued a little later under the title *Architectural Parallels* in which he gives many large-scale drawings of mouldings from various sources.

§ 6. ON THE BUILDING OFFICERS

From a careful examination of the Calendars of Close, Patent, and other Rolls, in the course of which more than a thousand entries, extending over some three hundred years, have been extracted and considered, and also by data derived from various other sources, the following notes have been obtained. The instances given are, however, only a selection taken to indicate the names of persons and offices and the duties performed in them throughout the centuries; they are also intended to show the control and administration of building works in connexion with which definite royal and other commissions or appointments, &c., were held.

The dualities of office—and even more complex appointments —that were sometimes held by one person makes analysis difficult. For example, a *clerk of works* might also be a *purveyor* or a *controller of works* or a *keeper of works*; or works might be to his ' view and testimony ' either as to their need or their execution, in which case he would be called a *viewer*, and so on. It often, therefore, becomes difficult to determine precisely where one office left off and another commenced. At other times discrimination is clearer; as for instance, when Bishop Wykeham commenced restoration works at Winchester, about 1394, he definitely appointed William Wynford as designer and architect (*dispositor et ordinator*) and (*Dominus*) Simon Membury as *supervisor . . . et solutor*, under him (or mayhap, over him), while John Wayte was named by the Convent as *controller* (*contrarotulator*),[2] but as no clerk of works

---

[1] *Architectural Nomenclature of the Middle Ages*, Cambridge Society's Trans., vol. i, 1840–6.

[2] Notes of Congress of the British Archaeol. Association at Winchester, 1845.

is mentioned, probably Membury also officiated as such, and there is no question but that he was a cleric.

Taking the offices mentioned in various records, there is first the much debated question of the ' architect '.

1. **The Architect**.

If any person other than the master-mason may at all be claimed as *architect* amongst the various officials in building affairs, it would appear almost safest to consider the *devisor* as such person ; but even then only in a very limited sense, and rather as a person who generally directed affairs than one who designed building work artistically or constructively.   This term does not often occur. Henry Yevele (*c.* 1360) at Westminster and John of Padua (1544–9) were referred to as such [1] (though they were primarily master-masons).   There are also one or two other like references, but in most cases they are of quite late date when the idea of such a person as an architect was arising.[2]

The fact, however, is that in mediaeval days the only person to whom the title ' architect ' could be applied with any sort of recti-tude was the master-mason.   At first he usually served in the actual labours of the work in hand as well as in a directive capacity, and it was not until the very latest period that he could have occupied any position approximating that which is known to-day.   The architect, however, had become established as a professional man by the date of the Renaissance, and while for a time thereafter he still dealt consistently with architecture, in its so-called rebirth, in the current and essentially Italian manner, he became at length a mere purveyor of styles in design.

In the twelfth, thirteenth, and fourteenth centuries the term *ingeniator* [3] is often found.   This office is a little obscure, but it appears to have carried a sort of general responsibility for any work in hand as a whole, and probably for the design of it.

---

[1] A French instance is recorded ' Frere Jehan Jocundus, religieux de l'ordre de S. Françoys, diviseur des bâtimens ; 1497 '. *Bulletin*, Comité Historique des Arts, 1843, i. 168.

[2] Lanfred, who built the Castle of Ivry (Normandy) in the twelfth century (and was said to have been put to death afterwards in case he should build a better for some other employer), was called an architect by Orderic Vitalis. Morter, *Recueil des Textes*.

[3] Some have held that such a man was practically the architect, nevertheless there is a strong presupposition that the word refers to military officers chiefly.

The following are a few of the instances on record :

1160. **Ailnothus,** *ingeniator.* Probably a military architect also. He was paid sundry monies.[1] He appears to have been working at Westminster Palace from 9 to 24 Hen. II and was styled by this name. His name occurs till about 1174.

1170. **Ricardus,** *ingeniator.*[2] ' . . . vir artifiosus . . . et prudens architectus in omne structura '.[3] He was employed by Bishop Pudsey at Norham Castle ; he doubtless did military engineering work also. He was probably succeeded by William who, in 1197, is also recorded at Norham.

1199. **Elyas,** *ingeniator.* Employed on the repair of the King's Houses at Westminster (10 Rich. I). Walpole's *Anecdotes* cites a writ mentioning this man and refers to a predecessor in the same office, but does not name him.

1206. **Peter,** *ingeniator.* Was at the Tower of London ; he was paid 9d. a day, an unusual wage.

1256. **Gerard** (Master), *ingeniator.* This seems to be an actual instance of the King's engineer as a military officer (40 Hen. III).

1275. **Richard** (Master), *ingeniator.* Several times mentioned in connexion with work at Chester Mills ; later he was at Conway Castle also, and received with Henry de Oxford (called a carpenter) £100 for carpentry work there. He is mentioned again in 1296 as receiving 12d. a day (26 Ed. I), finally confirmed for life.[4]

1299. **Robertus de Ulmo** (Frater), *ingeniator,* and also *magister.* He was paid 12d. per diem.

1300. **Thomas de Hokyntone,** *ingenarius.* This man worked on the tomb for Queen Eleanor which John de Convers made, and who was paid v marks for so doing.

The master-mason was unquestionably in existence throughout all this period ; he may have acted under or with the *ingeniator*, but when the term disappears (which it certainly does, c. 1300, from the Rolls records at least) there only remains the 'master-mason', who, as already stated, was the official to whom alone the term architect could be applied. The 'master-carpenter', for all works of timber, was usually quite an independent person, as also were the 'masters' in other trades.[5] In rare instances the 'clerk of works' may have acted in some limited way as an architect, though it is very doubtful.

---

[1] Pipe Rolls : three entries ; xls. ; xl. xiis. xid. ; and xl. xiis. xid., being paid to him in part ' pro operiendo refectoris '.

[2] So called in a charter in connexion with an exchange of land. Papworth, op. cit.

[3] *architectus* surely means nothing more here than ' chief builder '.

[4] His wages were in arrear towards the end of the reign of Edward I, and by 1 Edw. II an order was issued to pay him 18l. 4s. of monies due.

[5] See the later notes on the 'Masters', pp. 52-60.

2. **The Supervisor** (or Surveyor).

The services of this official are, like many others, often vague and uncertain. The *surveyor* might be a person dealing with quite other affairs than building operations. Persons who dealt with the administration of properties and other concerns of royal or civil import were so styled. They seem to have been more like 'inspectors' or 'reporters' in matters of building—as to work necessary to be done or on matters in the doing, or as to the completion of work. Sometimes the term is used so as to imply a certain amount of directive control, but it is very improbable that such ever extended to matters of design or construction, for persons of obviously non-technical knowledge held appointments from time to time.

The term persists throughout a very long period, and towards the end of it the office became quite a different one to that of the earlier days ; at length it was applied to such men as Inigo Jones and Sir Christopher Wren, both of whom were architects almost exactly in the same capacity as modern men.[1]

In 1100 **Alduin de Malverne,** *surveyor*, had to deal with matters concerning a bridge at Hereford. His name occurs till as late as 1135.

In later twelfth and thirteenth century entries in the Rolls reference is more often to *keepers of works* and *viewers*, and the term *surveyor* rarely occurs, but in the later centuries there are :

1308. **John Frounceys** (Master) and another ; appointed to survey and report on the state of the houses, &c., belonging to the brotherhood of the free chapel of St. Martin-le-Grand, and to inquire also as to moneys, if any, received for repairs thereto.

1313. **John de Norton,** *surveyor*; commanded (7 Ed. II) to purvey materials for the Palace of Westminster and the Tower of London.

1315. **William de Shaldeford,** *surveyor*, &c.[2] By 9 Ed. II this man is appointed to be : (a) *controller* of the 'chamberlainship' of North Wales ; (b) *clerk of works* of 'Kaernervan' Castle ; (c) *surveyor of the works* in the King's castles of North Wales—three offices held by one man.

1334. **Richard de Sleford** (Master, Canon of Chichester) and others ; to survey losses and dilapidations, &c., at the Chapel of 'Hastynges' due to the misconduct of prebendaries and ministers there.

---

[1] Mr. Papworth, op. cit., thinks the names *supervisor* and *surveyor* are the same, the former being superseded by the latter as the time went on ; he also thinks that they are synonymous with the term *overseer* which frequently occurs in the records.

[2] See 'Clerk of Works', p. 50, et. seq.

1336. **John de Thyngden**; *surveyor of works* at the King's castle at
Newcastle-upon-Tyne, at a wage of 3*s.* a day. A very high
wage and without reason assigned.

1337. **John Boyfield,** *surveyor.* At Gloucester, where he continued
to act for some years and in 1377 became Abbot of the
house there. His successor completed the choir vault and
other works which Boyfield had commenced.

1342. **John de Faucomberge** and others ; to survey ' Scardeburg '
(*Scarborough*) Castle and report on repairs and to say ' how
much these will cost '.

1346. **John Walerand** (Brother), *surveyor*, and with another man as
controller of the King's works at Westminster, to purvey
materials. Also jointly with one Master William de
Rameseye, a mason, and with Master William de Aurley,
a carpenter, to obtain workmen in their respective trades.

1347. **Peter de Brugge,** *clerk and surveyor* of the King's works at
Westminster and the Tower.

1350. **Richard de Rothele,** *clerk and surveyor* of the King's works ;
to take workmen and get materials, and to bring back
absentee workmen, &c. ; with wages at 12*d.* when at the
works, and 2*s.* a day when attending to the King's business
elsewhere (other appointments at like wages occur).

1356. **Gilbert de Whitele,** ' *to survey* all carpenters, masons, smiths,
artillers, and other workmen and the work done by them '—
' to remove . . . any . . . unskilful in the works and replace
them and to do all things pertaining to the office (of
surveyor) with a wage of £40 yearly '.

—   **William de Wykham,**[1] *surveyor*, with all powers as to finding
men and materials. Afterwards he was appointed *chief
keeper and surveyor* and *clerk of works* (' capitalem custo-
dem et supervisorem castrorum regis ') at 12*d.* a day. As
he rose in royal esteem many other preferments were received by him and finally he became Bishop of Winchester.
He was succeeded by William Mulsho [2] in such office (q. v.).

1371. **John Wortyng,** to *survey* and *control* all purchases and purveyances of stone, &c., to make payments of workmen's
wages and other outlays and to certify the account of
Robert de Sibthorp, ' clerk of the said works '.

1380. **William de Basynges** (Master). Master of the hospital of
St. Mary, Strood ; appointed *chief surveyor and clerk of
works* of certain castles, to purvey men and materials and
do works under the survey and control of Hugh Herland—
at 12*d.* daily.

1384. —— ——. Richard II made his ' chamberlain of Berwick '
not only *clerk of works* but also ' keeper of the victuals
and artillery ' : the connexion between these duties seems
a little remote.

---

[1] See p. 50. In his earlier and lay-days Wykeham must really be considered to have been an *architect*. He was certainly so employed, and he was
not a master-mason. Later he had his own architect ; see Wynford, p. 55.
See also various authors on the *Life of Wykeham*.

[2] See also ' Clerk of Works ', p. 50.

1389. **Robert Hertele** and another ; appointed to control and survey general works and repairs at various places ; the constable of Windsor Castle to provide men and materials, with powers of arrest.

1413. **Thomas Tikhill,** *chief steward and surveyor.* Generally over the King's properties throughout the kingdom. To have £20 a year and such daily expenses ' as may be agreed '.

1415. **Robert Welton** (one of the clerks of the Receipt of the Exchequer), to be *surveyor* of the construction of a bridge, to provide men and materials and with power to arrest.

1417. **Robert Rodyngton** (' the King's esquire '), *surveyor* to the making of the King's towers at ' Portesmouth' ; to provide, as in previous instances and with power to arrest, and also to sell residues of timber. The record reads : ' Notre amé Esquier Robert Rodyngton, *surveour* de la construction de noz Toures a Portesmouth ' ; in another appointment elsewhere reference is made to ' une *surveiore* de les oveignez de devf. chastell et villes deing Northgales.'

1417. —— ——. An order dated in this year required ' sum gud, true, suffesaiunt mon, to be *surviour* of vitel and werkes in North Wales '. This seems an extraordinary appointment.

1426. **William Sevenok** and others, to be *surveyors* ' personally or by deputy ' for the King's works, to provide as before, with powers of imprisoning in cases of contumacy, and of holding inquisitions should any materials be taken away or purloined.

1439. **William Morton** (chaplain) to be *surveyor* of works at Calais, its harbour, wharf, and the necessary waterside works there.[1]

1445. **Robert Wheteley ;** appointed not only to be *surveyor* but *chief carpenter and disposer of works* [2] at Westminster and the Tower ; to have £20 a year and a robe annually ' as the esquires of the Household have '.

1472. **John, Lord le Scrope;** *surveyor* of the King's houses, &c., in rebuilding and repair after fire ; grant is made to him for life of £25 yearly (being a rent).

1474. **Richard Beauchamp** (Bishop of Salisbury) ; to be ' master and *supervisor of the works* of St. George's Chapel', Windsor, which was then being built. Sir Reginald Bray followed him and was also so styled. The bishop was also appointed as *master of the works* at Eton, but he was obviously not the designer.[3]

[1] What could a chaplain know of such ? Surely this and other references to further unlikely people go to show that the surveyor, more often than not, was a non-technical person, and that trained knowledge in building works was not essential to the holding of the office.

[2] Here is evidently a man of training in structural matters, and with his office of *surveyor* these other appointments are given him. It almost suggests that the surveyor was a person who held dominant control as to what was or was not to be done. [3] See p. 60.

1489. **Prior of Lanthony** (the King's chaplain) ; *surveyor* of repairs to a highway near Gloucester. To purvey men and materials and to have ' all small stones and fragments of stones and plaster from Gloucester Castle called ' lez rubbeys' except the squared stones called ' lez asshelers frestone ', for the road repairs.[1]

1514. **William Malverne**, *supervisor* at Gloucester Abbey. He was afterwards made Bishop of the See.

3. The Clerk of Works.

The office of clerk of works, *clericus operationum*, appears somewhat infrequently in later times because the masters in masonry, carpentry, plumber's and other works, or even other officers, seem to have been often appointed to include these with their respective duties.

The duties of the clerk of works may also have been involved under the office of the *custodes fabrica—custodes operarum—custos* of materials—' master of works ' or even treasurer or controller. The clerk of works often made, directed, or approved payments for labour or materials and occasionally purveyed both; altogether the details of this office are very much complicated.

In earlier times the clerk of works' wages were 2*d.* a day,[2] the same as was received by the ' *viewers* of the King's works ' and the castle watchman (Windsor).[3] He often held office there in conjunction with other appointments, as in 28 and 29 Edward I when John de Londonia was *constable* of the castle at Windsor (remuneration not stated) *and clerk of works* at 2*d.* a day, or Roger de Wyndsore, who was *janitor* of both gates at 4*d.* a day, *and clerk of works* at 2*d.* a day. Occasionally the clerk of works directly is mentioned as *purveyor* also and even as *surveyor*.[4]

The fifteenth-century contract for Fotheringhay Church (for the Duke of York) refers to ' the clerke of the werke ' as making payments for it in procedure.[5]

In the sixteenth century (if not before) this officer is occasionally found to have duties quite foreign to building work ; for instance, John Thorne (1570–1) is stated to have entered costs in his accounts (Compotus Rolls)—' for dighting forth wedes and making cleane the wyndowes . . . for pricking forth of songes at London . . . and . . . for a reame of fine paper . . .', &c., &c.

---

[1] So states the appointment. 5 Hen. VII.
[2] Many Close Roll entries give this wage. At later times it was regularly 12*d.* a day.   [3] 28 Edw. I, &c., &c.
[4] In 2 Hen. IV, William Denys has such appointment and also to obtain men and materials, with powers of arrest. Also 3 Hen. V, and other commissions.
[5] Papworth, op. cit.

In some of the Patent appointments the manifold duties of the clerk of works are specified with great clarity, as follows : [1]

1. To ' take ' [2] all the workmen necessary and set them to work.
2. To buy materials.
3. To pay for the above and carriage.
4. To pay wages.

   N.B. These payments are usually directed to be attested ' by view and testimony ' of the ' controller ' and the ' surveyor '.[3]

5. To bring back absentee workmen.
6. To arrest contrariants and commit them to prison.
7. To hold inquisitions for materials that had been eloigned.
8. To sell residues of trees provided for the works and to answer to the King for such sales.

The wage usually stated for these services was 12*d*. daily. To what extent the authority to ' set men to work ' may have included directions as to work itself is not quite clear. On the whole the clerk of works seems most often to have been a sort of general managing man in the business of works in hand.

Instances of appointments are as follows :

1241. The earliest mention is 25 Hen. III when a *clerk of works* was appointed to Windsor Castle. Later, in 1242 and 1244 are other references to this official.

1257. **John of Gloucester** [4] (Master) and another. To be *masters* of all works at castles, &c. John was a mason and his companion in office a carpenter. They also provided materials and men and were to be ' viewers ' and had a mandate to the ' sheriffs, constables and other keepers of the said works to be aiding them '.

1266. **Robert de Beverle** and others. *Keepers* of the King's works, In 1276 Beverley (Beverlaco) had £202 19s. 9d. for labour and materials. The details of payment are given but they amount only to £162 19s. 9d., leaving a balance of £40 unassigned. Other ' keeper ' appointments follow in succeeding years.

---

[1] Sometimes these duties were issued to surveyors, and occasionally even to entirely non-technical persons.

[2] i. e. to impress ; this was the customary procedure in the case of Royal works, there was no option as to the King's requirements, and imprisonment was the only alternative. Cf. mandate of Edward III, 1353. London Letter Book G., fol. x.

[3] This was not invariable; 50 Edw. III directs Robert Coke, a *chaplain*, to attest ' by view, testimony and controlment ', and again in the next year, when William Hannay was clerk of works at ' Haddele ' Castle, but in this case the ' surveyor ' also attested.

[4] See also p. 54.

1284. —— ——. Appointment of a *clerk of works* at Carnarvon Castle. Wages 8*d.* a day while the 'master of works' received 2*s.* 2*d.* daily.[1]

1315. **William de Shaldeford,** *clerk of works.* This is the first direct mention of a clerk of works in the Patent Rolls.[2]

1331. **Walter de Weston,** *clerk of works.* At the Tower of London and Westminster Palace ' Clericus operationum domini ', later described as ' custos operationum '. In 1349 he was made royal chaplain and granted one-sixth of a prebend in St. Stephen's Chapel.

1347. **Peter de Brugge,** *clerk* and *surveyor.*[3]

1356. **William de Wykeham,** *clerk of works.*[4] There are many entries of appointments held by this man and some of special preferment in recognition of the royal esteem in which he was held ; in some of his appointments the terms *clerk of works* and *surveyor* are both used.

1358. **John de Rouceby,** *clerk* and *surveyor* at the manor of Eltham at 12*d.* a day ; and to purvey men and materials (see below).

1361. **William Mulsho,** *clerk of works,* with considerable managerial powers, including those of purveyance of men and materials and of arrest. Wages 6*d.* a day. Later in the same year another clerk of works was appointed at another place at 12*d.* a day. In November of the year he was directed to pay the surveyor, John de Rouceby, who was then appointed also to various positions other than at Eltham, which he then held, at the rate of 6*d.* a day.[5] Frequent other references to Mulsho occur at later dates.

1365. **Adam de Hertyngdon,** *clerk of works.* At Wyndesore Castle, manor, and park, and elsewhere. The appointment specifies many duties and powers : to take men and materials, to pay wages and for materials, &c., to account for monies received, to reclaim unlicenced absentees and to imprison, to inquire ' by oath of good men ' for materials and to sell residues, and to have the same wages as his predecessor William Mulsho. Later appointments are given him elsewhere. He was made Canon of Windsor in 1370.

1367. **John** (Prior of Rochester) ; *chief master of works* at Rochester Castle ; specifies like duties and powers as Hertyngdon, and by ' view and testimony ' of William de Basynges, master of St. Mary's Hospital, Strood.[6] Later Basynges was appointed *clerk of works* to this castle and also to that

---

[1] This is an extraordinarily large wage and no special reason for it appears : it may have included travelling expenses and horse hire.

[2] See 'Surveyors' at this date, p. 45.

[3] Ibid., p. 46. See note 1, p. 51.   [4] Ibid., p. 46.

[5] See p. 46, 'Surveyors'. Reference is made in this appointment to William Wykeham as receiving a similar wage, but why these men had 6*d.* and others in the same year 12*d.* is by no means clear. They were both men of considerable standing.

[6] See 'Surveyors' under *Basynges*, p. 46.

at 'Ledes' (Kent), and other works; later still these appointments were extended and like duties and powers conferred as above, and at a wage of 12*d*. a day.

1375. **William Hannay,** *clerk of works*, at the manor of Haveryng-atte-Boure. Duties and powers as before. The next year his rewards are stated as ' such wages daily and in such manner as the clerks of such works take ', and later still (when he is also called *controller*), at 12*d*. a day. In 1399, 22 Rich. II, mention is made of a grant for life which the late Hannay held as a prebendary[1] at Westminster, which preferment is thereby given to John Godmeston, *clerk of works*, at Westminster Palace.

1382. **Arnold Brocas,** *clerk of works*, at Westminster, the Tower, Windsor, and elsewhere. He seems to have been also sculptor and painter.[2] He was a very important man and many entries refer to him.

1390. **Geoffrey Chaucer**[3] (the King's esquire), *clerk of works* at St. George's Chapel, Wyndesore Castle, 'which is ready to fall into ruin ', to repair it, to choose workmen and obtain materials and with powers of arrest.

1391. **John Gedeney,** *clerk of works*; for various works and for a bridge at ' Rouchestre '; with general powers to purvey men and materials. He had a grant of cloth for a gown of livery. William Hannay was appointed at the same time as *controller*.

1423. **John Arderne,** *clerk of works*, at Westminster and the Tower, with the usual wages, rewards, and other profits. Later, William Pakyn was appointed as his deputy. Arderne from time to time issued bills of appointment to sundry persons to survey work and to purvey men and materials, &c. He worked on the tomb of Henry V. He also had a livery.

1441. **William Lynde,** *clerk of works*, at Eton College; appointed to arrest and provide men 'any previous arrest of such workmen for the King or any other person notwithstanding '; to provide materials and carriage for the same; with powers of imprisonment, and of inquisition as to materials removed.

1460. **John Marshall** (Yeoman of the Chamber), *purveyor* and *clerk of works* at Clarendon ' with the usual fees, wages, and profits '. John Hurley was also so described in an appointment the same year at Portsmouth and elsewhere.

1472. **Thomas Hunte**, *clerk of works* at Westminster and the Tower and many other places, including the mews at ' Charyng-crouche ', &c., &c., a very wide appointment, and it was for life ; ' receiving the accustomed fees in the same manner as Thomas Stratton deceased '. The appointment is repeated in 1 Rich. III (1484).

---

[1] Originally a person receiving an allowance of food, &c., but later implying ecclesiastical office ; doubtless the former meaning here.

[2] Papworth, op. cit.   [3] The poet ! See his *Life*, Godwin, 1803, &c.

1502. **Henry Smyth,** *clerk of works* at Windsor Castle, was appointed additionally as ' keeper of the leads there ',[1] at 2*d.* a day.

1550. **Eustace Mascall,** *clerk of works* to Cardinal Wolsey, at St. Frideswide, Oxford. For seventeen years he was chief clerk of accounts for all the buildings of Henry VIII within twenty miles of London.[2]

4. The Masters.

The term 'master' (*magister*) was not confined by any means to the trade of the mason ; there were masters of carpenters, of plasterers, and of most of the allied building trades, just as there were also masters in all other trades. The master-mason is the most frequently mentioned in building affairs and the master-carpenter is the next, and these two represented the major building operations. Buildings of stone were generally in the charge of the former and those of wood of the latter. They were almost without exception lay-men, and such secular terms as *vir* or *artifex* were usually adopted in the records referring to them.

(a) *Masons.*

Of these instances have already been given [3] which generally cover the mediaeval period under review. To them, if to any, must the term *mediaeval builder* in any capacity as ' architect ' be applied. They were fully qualified trainees of the craft-guilds and in intimate connexion with them ; and many of them rose to positions of note both in their craft and in general esteem. They actually worked [4] with men of their lodges, doing some of the more difficult pieces themselves and setting-out and generally directing the work of others. Their wage was usually 12*d.*[5] a day, and the royal master-masons were frequently granted a robe, sometimes furred, once a year, and often other ' fees, rewards, and profits ' of various sorts, sometimes including lodging or ' herberage ', and food. These emoluments were occasionally conceded by the large monastic establishments to their master-masons ; at Durham, for example, in 1398 the master-mason had a cloth gown each year, a daily loaf of white bread, a gallon of ale, and a ' spitful of meat ' of the same

---

[1] Wright says the *leads* were the battlements. *Prov. Dict.*

[2] Papworth, op. cit.   [3] See *ante,* § 2, p. 10 *et seq.*

[4] A contract even so late as 1488 (Durham) defines that the mason, John Bell, ' shall give his due labour . . . and *bodily labour.* . . .'

[5] At Exeter (*c.* 1300) a lesser rate obtained ; entries in the Fabric Rolls give 6*d.* a day and even less. Master Roger, there, received 30*s. pro termino,* but how long that was is not stated. In some other instances also the 6*d.* rate is to be noted. Bonuses were also given at times.

quality as prepared for the table of the esquires.[1]   And frequently a yearly fee was paid to the masters additionally.

In the instances of contracting there were frequently clauses agreeing the supply of food, clothing, aprons, gloves, and even shoes as part of the remuneration of the work.[2]

One of the earliest uses of the word ' master ' occurs in 1127 when one Andrew was *cementarius* at St. Paul's and was doubtless a ' master ',[3] the next mention is of *Magister Robertus, cementarius* in connexion with Westminster, and afterwards the term is in frequent use.

There is a long sequence of master-masons to be noted at Westminster Abbey.[4]   The earliest, Master Henry of Westminster, from 1244 to 1253 and following on throughout the years into the fifteenth century to Sir Richard Whittington in 1413 and John Colchester two years later.   This last named afterwards went to York, where he was subjected to considerable hostility in the lodge because he intercepted the seniority of succession among the masons there, and so acute did this trouble become that it was necessary to make special appeal to the Chapter to save him from serious personal violence.

There is also a considerable list of the master-masons employed at Windsor Castle.[5]   See also the masons mentioned in the various contracts already cited,[6] and as follows :

1113. **Arnold.**[7]   A lay-brother at Croyland Abbey.   He was much esteemed for his alleged abilities in building, but there is no doubt that some of his work failed badly.

---

[1] York Fabric Rolls, &c., give other instances.   The workmen also were fed in some cases and their wages adjusted accordingly.   Wages in the fifteenth century (1443), 23 Hen. VI, may be noted in a Petition which proposed, *inter alia*, that : ' a Maister Tyler or Sclatter, rough-Mason, and meen Carpenter and other Artificiers concernying beldyng, by the day iij*d.* with mete and drynk and without mete and drynk iiij½*d.* (winter time). . . . Tyler, meen Carpenter, rough-Mason, and other Artificers aforesaid, by the day ij½*d.* if with mete and drynk, withoute . . . iiij*d.* and every other Werkeman and Laborer by the day i½*d.* if with mete and drynk, and without mete and drynk . . . iij*d.*, and who that lasse deserveth, to take lasse . . .' *Antiquarian Reports*, 1808, iii. 53.   See also *Rot. Parl. m.* 4, *No.* 19.

[2] See a Westminster contract (1350) and those for the Walberswick Steeple (1426) and the Bell Tower at Bury St. Edmund's (1435), the altar front at Wells (1470), St. George's Chapel, Windsor (1474), and many others (14th, 15th, and 16th cent.) for similar provisions.

[3] Lethaby, op. cit.   [4] Ibid., p. 150 et seq.

[5] See St. John Hope's *Windsor Castle*, which contains also many interesting notes on the building matters there.

[6] See § 3, p. 28 et seq.   [7] See p. 19.

1174. **William of Sens** (already mentioned), and also William the Englishman who succeeded Sens at Canterbury. The later William has been identified by some at Coventry as designer of the great church there—they say his name was William of Coventry.

1189. **Gaufridus de Noiers** of Lincoln ' nobilis fabricae constructor '. Lincoln choir is attributed to him. He was a great man !

1200. **Hugh de Goldcliff** (already mentioned at Bury St. Edmunds) ; he was not a man of great integrity whatever may have been his abilities as a mason.

1200. **Elyas de Derham** ; chiefly concerned with the building of Salisbury Cathedral (1220–45) of which he was a canon. He was associated with one Robert who was there for twenty-five years (1217–42) and who was probably the actual master-mason. Elyas was called ' rector' of the work.[1]

1255. **John of Gloucester.** He worked for the king at Gloucester and elsewhere and was granted ' two robes with furs of good squirrels yearly for life '. He later held other important appointments and also at Westminster (1257–60) where he succeeded Master Albericus.

1291. **Richard de Stow.** He executed the Eleanor Cross at Lincoln, and possibly some other of those memorials. On these William de Hibernia did some of the sculpture.[2]

1324. **Roger Alomaly.** He apparently then met his death in some fracas with the monks at Westminster and an inquiry was directed.

1330. **Thomas of Canterbury.** Worked at St. Stephen's Chapel, Westminster ; also at Guildhall Chapel in 1352.

1351. **William de Hoton** (Master). There were two men of this name at York, the senior followed Master Thomas de Patenham, and he worked there for many years and when he was considered too old to continue in office, his son William junior was appointed by the Chapter by the indenture dated 1st October, 1351. Reference is made as to the skill and industry of the father and a grant was made him in consequence of £10 of silver yearly and the dwelling that his predecessor Patenham had.[3]

1359. **Geoffrey de Carleton.** Appointed to the works at Windsor to have 6d. a day and for his robe and for shoe leather 20s. a year.

1367. **Peter Mason.** A well-esteemed alabaster mason ; he made ' a great table of alabaustre ' at ' Notyngham [4] for the King's Chapel at Wyndesore '. It took more than a fort-

---

[1] ' Robertus cementarius rexit per vigintiquinque annos.' *Leland.*

[2] John de Bello executed the crosses at Stony Stratford, Northampton, and elsewhere, and Alexander *le Imaginator* carved the figures on several of them. See *Archaeologia*, vol. xxix, pp. 167–91.   [3] See *ante*, p. 21.

[4] Nottingham was a noted place for alabaster work in the Middle Ages. Large quantities were quarried in Derbyshire. Of what this ' table ' consisted is not quite clear, probably it was the whole of the high altar and reredos for St. George's Chapel.

night to bring this ' table ' to London, and all men, carts, and horses required were directed to be taken by the sheriff of ' Notyngham ' and others, with orders to imprison contrariant owners.

1369. **William de Wynford** (Master). Although Wynford is not recorded as an architect he might almost be classed amongst them. He was a master-mason, but there is little doubt that he served in the former capacity. In 1375 he was at Abingdon [1] and he had a furred robe, the fur of which cost 2s. 10d. He was appointed under Bishop William de Wykeham's will to have charge and to direct the works at Winchester Cathedral. His portrait is to be found in one of the windows of the College there. He stood very high in Royal esteem (see 45 and 46 Ed. III, &c.). He was paid 12d. a day and had certain additional emoluments of office, and also sundry grants of farms and other properties for life from the King.

1392. **Robert de Skyllyngton** ; was evidently employed at Kenilworth Castle, for he found men to work there.

1398. **John de Middleton.** Contracted for Durham dormitory which was completed by Peter Dryng in 1401, and two other masons, Robert Daynwell and William Landes, also worked on it.

1399. **Robert Fagan** (Master). Appointed to take labourers of his ' mistery ', and set them to work for the King.

1400. **Stephen Lote.** Worked at Westminster and the Tower, at 12d. a day and ' a winter robe yearly '. Was associated with Henry de Yevele in work and in private life.[2]

1416. **Thomas Hyndeley.** Did part of the cloister at Durham. Thomas Mapilton (1413) and John Fethyrstanhalgh also worked at Durham.

1435. **John Wode.** Contracted for the Tower at Bury St. Edmund's Abbey.

1439. **Robert Westerley**, *mason* ; the King's serjeant. To have 12d. a day and an allowance for his expenses (claimed under oath) when riding or otherwise.

1445. **Richard Beck** (Master) ; was appointed at Canterbury, having 4s. a week and a house, &c. He was consulted later as to the stability of the arches of London Bridge ; he was evidently a man of considerable note.

1470. **John Stowell,** called a ' ffreemason '. Contracted for an altar front in St. Cuthbert's Church at Wells.

1475. **William Orcheyard**. Contracted for a considerable part of Magdalen College, Oxford.

For further names and other notes see the master-masons mentioned earlier in this book §§ 2 and 3.

In the sixteenth century work was usually done by contract and the master-mason agreed to carry it out to a design and specification he supplied, or to an approved model, or by reference to existing

---

[1] *Abingdon Accounts*, Camden Society, 1892.   [2] See p. 56.

work as defining what was intended to be done. The architect or surveyor at this period was becoming more essential to building enterprises, but there were many instances wherein the master-mason or other artificer still continued to supply work without any such interposition.

From 1356–1400 one of the greatest masters of masons was **Henry de Yevele** ; to him there are frequent references in the Patent, Exchequer, and other Rolls. In 1356 he had no higher title than 'mason hewer', but he rose rapidly in fame and royal favour. He worked chiefly at Westminster Abbey,[1] where in 1362 he was styled the 'devisor of masonry'. He appears to have remained at the Abbey until his death at the age of eighty years, in 1399, though he was also engaged on or consulted about many other works, amongst which the Guildhall, London, was designed by him.

Some of these master-masons and the masters in other trades also were men who were held in high esteem, particularly those who were connected with royal affairs.[2] They often possessed considerable property. Yevele was a 'citezein' of London and was a man of substance as well as of repute. In 1369 he was granted a robe equal to those of the esquires of the Household, for he was appointed to the service of the Crown in 1360.[3] He held the tenancy of the manor of Langstone in 'Purbike' in 1376.[4] He was confirmed in the possession of two shops in St. Martin's in 1383.[5] Later he received the manors of Tremworth and Vannes (co. Kent).[6] He was buried in St. Magnus Church, London Bridge, in 1400, and Stowe in his *Survey* said the monument was to '*Henry Yeuele*, Free Mason to *Edward* the Third, *Richard* the Second, and *Henry* the Fourth'.[7] He left endowments for two chantry priests, and his will[8] speaks of his own residence called 'La Gleve', in St. Magnus parish, which he devised to his (second) wife Katherine, and also other properties, land, and houses in London and Essex.

Another, and earlier evidence of the importance of a mason may be gathered from the fact that Walter Dixi *cementarius de Bernewelle* in 1277 had lands to convey. This he did to his son Lawrence ;

---

[1] It is remarkable that the nave, on which he was largely employed—even in its design as some say—shows such consistent treatment despite the fact that architectural style had moved onward far towards the *perpendicular*. This fact evidences the control of the work by a single mind.

[2] It is even recorded that Henry III exchanged wine with John of Gloucester, who was his mason at Westminster at the time.

[3] Lethaby, op. cit.   [4] *Placita de Quo Warranto*, p. 181.

[5] Harl. Charters, 43 E. 28.   [6] Pat. Rolls, 43 Edw. III.

[7] *Survey of London*, 1598. Strype edit. 1720, bk. 2, p. 174.

[8] Hustings Roll, 1 Henry IV, memb. 3.

the seal attached to the deed bore the motto : ' S^g Walter le Masun ' and a monogram.[1]

An interesting appreciation, though late in date, is to be found in a York will ; speaking in memory of one Christopher Horner, mason, it says he was a man—' myghtie of mynd and of a hool myndfulness '.[2]

These cases, given in this sub-section, may be generally taken as illustrative of the standing and recognition of master-masons— and while it is quite possible that some may prefer to consider, and perhaps quite rightly, that they were the practical equivalent of the architect of to-day in many of the aspects of his relationship, there is one point that must always be kept in mind, namely, that these men were *of a trade* rather than of a profession—they rose from abilities of craftsmanship to whatever administrative positions they held in later days, and insomuch the modern architect cannot be likened to them.

(b) *Carpenters.*

The master-carpenter is mentioned only a little less frequently than the master-mason. He was concerned with the houses of wood and the great timbered roofs and other wooden structures. His wage was often the same as the mason, but he seldom rose to the eminence of or obtained the rewards given to the latter.[3] In the Patent Rolls the first master-carpenter mentioned is in the thirteenth century, when :

1226. **Jordan** (Master), carpenter, was paid 30s. as a part payment for his livery.

1257. **Alexander,** chief master of all works of castles, &c., this side Trent and Humber, and to provide the ' carpenterie ' thereof.

1262. **Thomas Burnel.** Grant of 3d. a day as wages when succeeding his father Ralph who had the same. Later the grant was confirmed for life, but it stated that as he is 'not a carpenter, whereby he cannot fill the office ', the King nevertheless, in regard of the long service of the father, granted him of special grace ' the said 3d. a day for life '.

1284. **William de Trene.** Appointed carpenter of the King's houses in Ireland, with 12d. a day and 40s. a year for his robe.

1346. **William de Hurlee.**[4] Appointed as carpenter at Westminster

---

[1] *Archaeologia*, vol. xxx, p. 119, where a drawing is given.

[2] *Fabric Rolls*, Surtees, op. cit.

[3] In the Exeter Fabric Rolls, Master Walter, a carpenter, received (c. 1300) 2s. 3d. a week, and another carpenter 2s. 1d. These rates are lower than those given in the Patent Rolls, where 12d. a day is more usual.

[4] *Hurlee* may possibly be merely an error in spelling and *William Herland* was intended.

Palace. In 1352 he did some work at the Guildhall Chapel.

1360. **William Herland** (Master). Appointed to Westminster, the Tower, and elsewhere, and to find and engage men. In 1370 he was authorized to take eighty carpenters and with two other appointees, who were to take forty each, to bring them to London for the King's works as he ' shall please to assign them ' ; and with power of arrest.

In 1376 he was granted a tenement value 40s. yearly for long service, and four years later he died at an advanced age.

1364. **Hugh Herland.** Son of William, under whom he first worked as foreman. At this date he was granted 8d. a day on the Westminster works. Later he did the great roof of the Hall, for the carrying of which Yevele had prepared the stone-work. Elsewhere he is called *apparitor* of carpenters' work.

In 1375 he was appointed as ' disposer of the King's works touching the art or mistery of carpentry ' at Westminster and the Tower, at 12d. a day for wage and a ' winter robe yearly . . . of the suit of the esquires of the household or such sum as the esquires take therefor'. The Order[1] refers to the death of William Herland who also had a robe. This appointment was confirmed by the succeeding King, 1 Rich. II (1378),[2] and later he was reappointed on like terms, and the next year his wages are again stated at 12d. daily and the winter robe.[3] In 1391 he was granted for life 10 marks a year on certain stated conditions, and in 1396 a life-grant of ' a little house at Westminster ' wherein he kept his tools and made his models (*formulae*) and had so done for thirty years.

1365. **John de Gleymesford.** To take carpenters, sawers and hewers of stone, and other craftsmen for work at Wyndsore Castle, and with power to imprison the rebellious until the King should give order touching their punishment.

1391. **John Pykerell,** *master-carpenter* at Calais with the usual fees.

1403. **William Wyse,** *carpenter* at Windsor Castle and manor, &c. to have 6d. a day and robe of livery.

1421. **William Yerdhurst,** *master-carpenter*, to obtain men and materials for sundry royal works.

After this date the *chief carpenter* is more often mentioned, though *master* occurs from time to time.

(c) *Other Masters.*

There are a few appointments in the Rolls of other ' masters ' of trades allied to building, for example :

(1) **Joiners.** In 1417 Robert Cony was directed to take and deal

---

[1] In this Order he is called *Master*.

[2] Here—' carpenter and controller of works ' is his designation.

[3] In 1398–9 record gives Master Hugh as at the King's Great Hall and John of Godmeston as the clerk of works, keeping accounts which are attested by ' syght and testimony ' of Hugh.

with the men of his ' mistery of joignour ', in the making of small wood-work, chiefly furniture of sorts ; seven years later he is again referred to in like terms, and also in 1425. Joiners are seldom mentioned in early building affairs.[1]

(2) **Plumbers.** William Smyth, *plomber*, was appointed in 1376 to be King's plumber at a wage 12*d.* daily, which was stated to be as ' Robert Horwood deceased took '. In 1377 and in 1399 the appointment was confirmed.

In 1367 John Plomer of Blake Street, York, was appointed to do ' the plumber's work with his own hands and not by substitute ' at York Cathedral, and ' as he shall be required by the *master of the fabric* of the said church ' and to have ' two shillings and sixpence of silver for his stipend and for his labour, without requiring anything further ' ; and he took oath to fulfil his agreements and found a bond in 40 marks of silver as a surety.

Three years later a certain John de Beverley was appointed and it was required that after the melting of lead ' in his office ', such was ' to be cleaned of ashes, &c '. Other plumbers are mentioned in later records.[2]

In 1442 Richard Wolnothe was made ' serjeant of the King's plumbers ' and paid 12*d.* daily ; he had also a robe at Christmas and ' all the houses and dwelling-places to the office accustomed '.

In 1461 John Brycheold held the office at 12*d.* daily wage and other emoluments including a livery, or 40*s.* in lieu thereof, yearly. At Exeter in the fourteenth century a master-plumber had 6*d.* a day.[3]

(3) **Smiths.** Mention of one occurs in 1354, when Andrew le Fevre was appointed as *master-smith* at 8*d.* daily wage, and a ' robe befitting his estate . . . provided that he stay continually in that office in person and discharge it as it should be done '. In 1359 he was appointed to provide iron, steel, and charcoal for the work at the Tower and to find smiths and other workmen. No other instance concerning a smith occurs in the Patent Rolls until 1446 when John and Stephen Clampard, father and son, were appointed at the Tower at like wages to the master-mason with robes and other emoluments.[4]

---

[1] The joiner or *junctor* of the mediaeval period was not a man of any such direct connexion with the building trade as to-day. The modern cabinet-maker would better represent him, and it was not until a very late period that he came to hold anything like the present relationships.

[2] J. Browne, *History of York.*

[3] *Fabric Rolls*, Exeter.

[4] See Pat. Rolls, 24 Hen. VI.

(4) **Glaziers.** In 1412 Roger Gloucestre was appointed *serjeant* in the office of glazier at a 12*d*. daily wage.

By 19 Hen. VI (1440) John Prudde *glasyer* was appointed as King's glazier with such ' fees and wages as Roger Gloucestre had ' and all other ' appurtenant profits ', and a ' shedde ' called *the glasyer's logge*. He also had a gown each year at Christmas of the King's livery of the suit of the *serjeant of the works*.[1] John was again referred to in 1444 and his office confirmed with like emoluments as in 1440 ; in this Patent, the ' shade ' or ' logge ' was then stated as being 60 ft. in length and 20 ft. in breadth.

Thomas Bye, *citizen*, held this office in 1461 at a wage of 8*d*. daily and ' a coat of the King's livery ', and also had the same ' logge '.

(5) **Painters.** By 1 Hen. V, a King's painter was appointed ; doubtless he was a master, for he was to attend to all things ' pertaining to the mistery of painting '.

5. *General Names.*

Besides the officers already named there are certain others mentioned in relation to building work. Sometimes they can only have implied one or other of the better recognized appointments and their names merely casual variants due to the idea of the scribe.

(*a*) The **master of the works** (*magister operum*) was at times only another term for the *master-mason* or that of some other particular trade ; it is not a very frequent term. Late in the sixteenth century ' Maister of the Warkes, a deviser of buildyng, architector et architectus ' may be noted.[2] At one time, however, there seemed to be a clear differentiation between the *master of the works*, *keeper of the fabric*, and the *master-mason*, for *c.* 1367, York Rolls, each are specifically mentioned in the same document. Henry VI's will refers to such officials and directs that £50 per annum shall be paid to the ' masters of the works ' at King's and Eton Colleges : this hardly appears to imply masters of various trades. But Richard Beauchamp's (Bishop of Salisbury) position there, as such under the direction of the will, was only to take oversight and give assent to the work and proceedings and also to ' bee prive to all charges and expenses that shal bee expended about it '. In such office he cannot be supposed to have been concerned in design or actual constructive problems.

(*b*) The **keeper of the fabric** or of the works (*custos operationum*), may have been a trained official or otherwise. As to the latter, Odo

---

[1] *Serjeant of works* is a very rare term.
[2] Sir Thomas Elyot, *Dictionary*, 1538.

the goldsmith of Westminster, who was succeeded by his son Edward, may be cited (*c.* 1225), or John of Wisbech, a monk of Ely (*c.* 1349), who was *custos* of the Lady Chapel there. At York there were many *keepers* in the course of its history,[1] one of whom was a Vicar Choral. They received monies and made payments, and generally had custody of the work.

(*c*) The **disposer of the works** may probably have been only a variant for the official otherwise acting as *supervisor* or *controller* ; it may be found applied to the masters of masonry and carpentry.

(*d*) **Warden of the works**[2] (*gardein*) is also to be found, but with no direct evidence as to whether he may not have been a quite non-technical person, and almost implying it, for an esquire or other lay-person was occasionally appointed.

(*e*) **Purveyor** (*provisor*) occurs many times at both early and late dates ; and they were often given duties wholly apart from building affairs. The office may also be found coupled with other appointments. The services required were generally to purvey men, materials, and things of all sorts necessary for the building enterprises mentioned in the various Patents appointing ; at times they were empowered to pay for these purveyances. The wages, &c., are not often mentioned ; in 1378 John Pynson, holding office as regards works at Westminster and the Tower, had 4*d.* as a daily wage. Later in the same year another purveyor was paid 6*d.* a day and had a life-grant. Some of the men appointed in these offices were those whose knowledge of building work as a science or design as an art must have been very remote, for here also quite non-technical persons are often named.

The purveyor's duties were sometimes combined with those of the office of *surveyor* or of the *clerk of works* (both of whom found men and materials at times), but often it was an independent appointment and the *purveyor* had to find men and materials to be used under the control and direction of a superior officer.

(*f*) The **viewer** may have been another name for a minor sort of surveyor, and the appointments often imply such. The term is applied at times to lay officials (i. e. non-technical). Even a church-man, a friar, or a parson, or the ' clerk to the keeper of the ward-robe ', none of whom could have technical knowledge of building affairs, may be found among appointees, receiving, as usual to the office, a wage of 2*d.* a day.

---

[1] See *Fabric Rolls.*
[2] In 1439, Pat. Rolls, 17 Hen. VI, the term ' warden of the masonry' (*gardein de masonry*) occurs. In 1441, *warden* of the King's carpenters occurs.

(g) The term *serjeant* is also to be found in later times in connexion with the offices of the smith, the plumber, and of the glazier. It was a quite important appointment, for besides the wage paid (usually 12*d.* a day) a robe of livery was generally included as well as other emoluments.

§ 7. ON THE PROCEDURES, TOOLS, MATERIALS, COSTS, &c., IN THE MEDIAEVAL BUILDING TRADES

Much information as to building operations may be gathered from the various names and uses of the tools and materials of mediaeval times, and also from the methods of procedure, costs, wages, &c., &c., incidental to the trades.[1] These matters are dealt with generally here, and amongst them interesting origins of custom and survivals may be noted.

The actual materials used by the mediaeval builder differ but little from those of modern experience, but much interest attaches to the methods of their production, carriage, measurement, and valuation and the general usages in the trades concerned.

The first matter to be considered in any building enterprise was naturally that of the ground work. For the labours of this there were the usual tools, the spade, *bescha*,[2] or *vanga*, of the ordinary sort ; another spade was of triangular shape and called a *didal*, and yet another, a smaller one, a *spyddell*. Picks, *picoys*, of various sorts were used, and crowbars when required.   Excavation works themselves do not generally call for any special mention, but when the ground was bad they had recourse to stakes and cross-timbers, as some illustrations show, to stiffen the foundation works and to prevent slipping. If the sub-soil was very poor and soft they adopted pile-work ; *pylyng*[3] and planking were often used to maintain the sides of the trenches.[4]

---

[1] Some of the terms are ambiguous and others are capable of more than one meaning. They are all drawn from sources mentioned in the List of Authorities—Appendix II, which see.   Reference to the Illustrations and the notes thereto will add information. See § 9 and the Plates.

As to the period during which the words and terms here given may have been in current use, it is very hard to say. There are so many factors to be taken into consideration ; it seems impossible to claim more for them than an existence in general during the mediaeval period.

[2] The word in italics given in immediate connexion with the terms is as it occurs in various manuscripts, &c., and thus throughout.

[3] Rams for pile driving are mentioned in the London Bridge inventory of stores, ' two engines with three rammes for ramming piles '. Riley, *Memorials*.

[4] Speaking of the bogs and marshes about the Abbey of Croyland the chronicler, Stukeley, in his *Itinerary* says that the foundations were laid on

In many cases the foundation work was excellently well done, and in others equally badly. Sometimes the ranges of piers in arcades were erected off continuous wall-works below ground—this was so at Hereford, Lichfield, and elsewhere. At Durham some of the foundations extend to as much as 14 ft. down to the solid rock, and at York some depths were even greater. But in many places failures of superstructures were due to bad foundation work, and probably such may be part of the reason for the present alarming condition of Peterborough Cathedral.

Following the preparation of the ground came the work of the masons, and in connexion with these there are many interesting terms. The mason was called at one time a *cementarius* [1] or at another a *latomus* or *lathomus* ; [2] various classes of them are mentioned—rough-masons or mason-hewers; mason-cutters, who were termed in some records *cementarii cissores*, and mason-layers or setters, *cementarii positores*. Freestone masons—a *mestre mason de franche pere*, and the derived designation *freemason*—may also be frequently found after the thirteenth century. [3] The London Assize of 1212 has *cementarius*; another term was *marmorius*, [4] and yet another, *saxcidus*, but the most common and the one generally used was *cementarius*.

The quality of the masonry of the later times showed considerable improvement on that of the earlier. The former had thick mortar joints, and stone ashlar-work of but moderate quality, but in the later periods—the fifteenth century—mason-craft became a science in which with amazing temerity it dared to undertake such a wonderful structure as the roof of Henry VII's Chapel at Westminster.

' piles of wood drove into the ground with gravel and sand '. Gough says that several of these were found in the ruins of the eastern part of the Church and that they dated from the tenth century. *Hist. of Croyland*, p. 100.

[1] The term *cementarius* is to be found, according to T. Wright, as early as the eleventh century, ' *cimentarius, weal wyrhta* ', but he does not give the source of his quotation. *Vocabularies*, 1857.

[2] This was the later name. In a record of 1380 (Pat. Rolls) directions are given as to providing masons for a lodge in Windsor Park—*tot latomos tam latomos vocatos fremasons quam latomos positores*. Last of all the term *mason*, and often *freemason*, became general.

[3] In connexion with Westminster Hall, *c.* 1396, mention is made of *lathomos vocatos ffremaceons* and *lathomos vocatos ligiers*. The term ' freemason ' occurs from the end of the thirteenth century onwards, but cannot be correlated to that of modern mason-craft. It appears in 1376, according to Gould, op. cit., and has no previous Latin word ; but *freestone* or its Latin or Latin-French equivalent appeared as early as 1212. It is clear that the former was derived from the latter. Papworth, Coulton, and others take this view.

[4] More correctly a marble mason ; *liberi muratores* has also been noted.

Ashlar face-work was built up of worked *acheleys* or squared stones sometimes called *essicis* (Fr. *assise*) and had a proportion of *thrughe stanes* or bonders at intervals; these extended right through the wall thickness and were also known as *talstons* (Fr. *pierree de taille*) ; sometimes these bond-stones are named *parpain-asshelers*, whence the modern term ' perpends ' which is still in use. The in-fillings of walls within the ashlar casing was made up with rough stones called *raggs* or *royboyll*. This method of building, though not yet wholly fallen into desuetude, is never quite satisfactory and by no means was as they did it, and this has been shown by the frequent failure of early masonry work and the collapse of buildings ; they even went so far as to case and fill-in piers, arches, and small pieces of masonry on which considerable weights were concentrated, and did the work most carelessly.[1]

The rougher class of wall-work was of rubble or unsquared pieces of stone ; for this the Roman name seems to have continued, for it is called *incertum opus* in-some records, but that term may possibly apply also to the in-fillings of ashlar-faced walls.

The cutting-out of decayed stones and the insertion of new was called *pinnare* or *pynnyng*, and the raking and repointing of the joints, *punctuacio*.

When it was necessary to take out considerable portions of old work, resort to *pynnyng* or underpinning, *growndepynnyng*, had to be made. The posts supporting this work were called *stodes*.

For the various portions of the mason work there were names of very modern form and sound : for example, the jamb-stones of the door or windows were called *jamwys* or *jawners*, and the seatings of window mullions, *monielles*, were *stooles*.[2]

Shaped stones were worked by means of *fourmers* or templates, *templez*, and *squirrae* or squares were used to set out work and others to fix it, some having a plumb-bob and line, *pedicula*, much after the form of the Roman tool for that purpose.[3]

---

[1] The present (1925) trouble in connexion with St. Paul's Cathedral is in part unquestionably due to this method of construction, though that work was much better done under the architects of the seventeenth century. How bad this was in the nave piers of Old St. Paul's may be noted from a report of Sir Christopher Wren himself, who said : ' they were only cased without and that with small stones, not one greater than a Man's Burden ; but within is nothing but a Core of small Rubbishstone and much Mortar, which easily crushes and yields to the weight.' See Bond's *Architecture*, op. cit.

[2] For further notes on *Nomenclature* see Willis, op. cit.

[3] See ' Illustration and Notes ' thereon, § 9, p. 88 et seq.

The master-mason set out his work with the *virga geometralis,* a measuring rod of about two yards in length. The *metrod* or *metwand* was another instrument of the same sort and was often fitted with two more or less ornamental terminals. By a careful system of identification marks cut on the stones the master-mason had an opportunity of considering the work of the various men under him and of checking their services, and for some such practical reason, no doubt, 'mason marks' had their origin and at first possibly never meant anything more.[1]

It is safe to assume that they understood the value of bed-setting their stone-work and probably also of side-setting it in arches and overhung work, though they were not always heedful of so doing. They also knew the wisdom of using a lighter form of stone for infillings to vault panels where the weight was borne by the ribs, and, therefore, *creta ad pendentia* is mentioned.[2]

Stone and wood carved work was done apparently both by the mason and by a special carver. *Sculptores lapidum liberorum* is given in the London Assize. William de Lyndeseye 'carver of wooden images in London' is referred to in the Issue Roll of 1367, being paid for making ' a certain table with images ' for Windsor.[3]

The term often used for the carver was the *entayler* or *intailer.* Mention of such is to be found in the fifteenth and sixteenth centuries at York.[4] One workman and his servant received 1*l.* 16*s.* in 1504, for six weeks' work, that is 12*d.* a day between them. As there are but rare references to such men in the earlier records, it suggests that then the mason often included carving work among his services.[5] The term *ymaginator* is also used but usually meaning the sculptor of figures.

---

[1] Probably some will raise considerable outcry against so prosaic an opinion as to ' mason marks ', nevertheless it is certainly open to such simple explanation—and simple explanations are not often far wrong, albeit the whole subject is full of interest, see p. 41. Other trades also used marks, the Carpenters and the Coopers, and they are well enough known in certain metal trades even into modern times.

[2] As early as the twelfth century such light stone is mentioned in connexion with the rebuilding of Canterbury Choir : *ex lapide et tofo levi* (Chron. Gervase), which refers to the use of *tufa,* a porous form of limestone. Bredon Church porch (Worcs.) is vaulted with this sort of stone.

[3] Exchequer Rolls, 40 Edw. III.

[4] *Fabric Rolls* : ' Jacobo Dam, pro intailyng clxxv crokettes 14*s.* 7*d.* for the screen ', 1478–9. The word is used there as late as 1535.

[5] 50 Edw. III : ' To John Orchard, a stonemason of London, in money paid to him . . . for making divers images, in the likeness of angels, for the tomb of Phillippa, late Queen of England . . . 5*l.*' Issue Roll, 1377. In 1386 there are two other payments for other carved works and images, for which a further payment was made for painting them.

As to costs in stone work there are multitudinous references in many of the authorities quoted, but as an instance of the definite charges and expenses on a piece of work the fourteenth-century window which was inserted in the Cathedral at Canterbury may be cited, when Henry de Estria was prior of the house. The window still exists; it is a large one, 17 ft. across its five lights with an elaborate traceried head of the period. The centre light is 3 ft. wide and the side 2 ft. 6 in. in the clear between the mullions.

'*Memorand. Quod anno 1336 facta fuit una fenestra nova in Ecclesia Christi Cant. viz. in capella SS. Petri et Pauli apostolorum, pro quo expensae fuerant ministratae—*

	l.	*s.*	*d.*
pro solo Artificio seu labore cementariorum	*xxi.*	*xvij.*	*ix.*
pro muri fractione ubi est fenestra		*xij.*	*ix.*
pro sabulo et calce		*xx.*	
pro M. M. ferri empti ad dictam fenestram		*lxxxiv.*	
pro artificio Fabrorum		*lxv.*	*iv.*
pro lapidibus Cani emptis ad eandem		*c.*	
pro vitro et labore vitraii	*vi.*	*xiij.*	*iv.*

Summa viij l. xiiij s. iv d. data fuit a quibusdam amicis ad dictam fenestram. Reliqua pecunia ministrata fuit a Priore.' [1]

As will have been already noted, the master-mason received 12*d.* a day and in many cases additional emoluments. The ordinary mason's wage was 5*d.* in 1281 (Newgate Gaol). In 1300 the Exeter masons got 6*d.*, and in the fifteenth century the rates were generally lower. Winter wages were usually reduced by about 25 per cent.[2]

The quarry whence the stone was obtained was known by several names, the *lapicidium*, the *petraria*, the *quarruria*, and the *standelf*,[3] amongst others. The quarry-man was called the *quarrerius* or *querrour*, and his general assemblage of tool the *hernas*. These tools included crowbars, *gaveloks*, and levers, *levators*, picks of various sorts: one had an end forged to a point and the opposite end blunt like a hammer, it was called an *assisculus*; with such a pick the *batiryng* or dressing of the stone was done. They had also a *besacia* or double-headed pick, a *brochaxe* to furrow the stone face, which was also done with a *broaching* chisel or *puncheon*. Dressing stone was also termed *dighting*.

They had a heavy *polaxe*, which weighed about 16½ lb., for breaking large stones, and a *pulipike*—a somewhat uncertain form of

---

[1] *Canterbury Cathedral*, vol. ii. Willis, who gives a drawing of the window.

[2] These rates must be generally considered as net, i. e. exclusive of food and drink which amounted in value to about 1¼*d.* or 1½*d.* more. See § 4, pp. 53–4.

[3] Though mentioned last, this was probably quite the earliest term.

implement—and also various *stanaxes*. A hammer-axe had one of its ends formed like a hammer and the other as an axe; it was a very similar tool to that still used in the Bath quarries to-day. A *quarel-mell* was a sort of large hammer—possibly of wood—used in the quarry. For cutting up stone they had sundry saws,[1] *sarrae*, and one called an *achetus* was among them (its specific form is obscure). *Wharelwegges* were wedges used in splitting stone.

They scabbled the block into rough shape with an axe; the operation was called *scablinge* or *scapellyng*, a term still in use, and they used *puncheons* and *celtes*, *chosels*, *chixills*—all names for chisels of sorts. There was another tool called a *perser* or *parsure*, but its form and use is uncertain. In working their stone they set it on a bench or *bancum*, whence the term 'banker' of to-day. When occasion required it, in fixing stone work they used *crampons* or dowels of iron, and these were of very similar shape to those of to-day—they were also called *clammys*. In setting they used *maliots* or *mauls* of wood, and what were called 'setting chisels', though what these were is not very clear.[2]

Various forms of hoisting tackle were used : the *rota* was one of them; it was a windlass and was also called a *wyndhuse*. As the heavier pieces of stone were lifted they were controlled by a guy-rope or *warderape*. Another sort of winding-gear and called a *ferne* and poles are mentioned in connexion with it. All these had the necessary *polys* or *puleyns* having sheaves or *shives* and ropes. The winding-drum was generally turned with spokes much of the same sort as those of the modern capstan.[3] To hold the blocks of stone they used *lowys* irons exactly like the 'lewis' of modern lifting tackle; they also had *cancers*, *pynsers* or *tenabulae*, and *stanhokes*, and these were like the tool of to-day having a pincer-like grip maintained by the pull of the chains as the weight was lifted. They had another hoisting arrangement called a *cancera*, a crab, and this, too, was much like the modern form of that appliance. At York ' a payre of tackells for wundinge ' is mentioned in the sixteenth-century *Accounts of the Clerk of Works*.

The smaller tools included *truls* trowels and hammers and mortar trays or hods called *bossys* and baskets, the former being made of

---

[1] In a MS. in the University Library, Cambridge, there is an illustration of two men sawing marble slabs with a *whip-saw*.

[2] See *Fabric Rolls*, York. Surtees, op. cit. pp. 17–18, for a detailed list of tools in the ' loge '.

[3] In the Accounts (*c.* 1480) at Kirby Muxloe Castle a cartwheel is mentioned as used in connexion with the *ferne* forming its turning wheel. Professor Thompson, *Leicester Archaeological Trans.*, 1924.

wood and were like long-shaped troughs, and were carried on the shoulder. Sometimes *barell' hedes* were used and a large tub, *coolle*, for holding it in bulk.[1]

For conveying stone from the quarry to the work various means were adopted; by sea in ships, or, if a river was available, it was used and barges loaded with stone; if not, then carts and horses [2] or horses alone were the only means possible, and it became a serious business.[3] For these horse-borne loads, and indeed very frequently for any loads, everything that could be done in the way of working down the rough blocks to finished sizes was done at the quarry itself, so as to reduce the weight to a minimum. For carrying the stone on horses, special panniers, *panyerys*, were used, which were slung on either side of the animal. It will, therefore, often be observable that where the transport of stone had to be done in this latter manner the stones in the building are never of any great cubic contents, weight precluding the use of large pieces—indeed, it has been reasonably suggested that the receding ' orders ' of arches, &c., were evolved by this necessity, as well as the economy in centerings.[4]

They contrived, however, to move considerable blocks of stone when necessary; the London Bridge Inventory of Stores, 1350, gives ' 18 great stones of " Bere ",[5] weighing altogether 18 tons, value 6s. 8d. per ton '.

Stone was valued by the ton—the *pondus*, equalling in measure about 40 ft. cube; it was also estimated by the ' load ' [6]—a somewhat doubtful measure, varying both in places and times—and by the foot cube, and occasionally where there were many pieces when worked of a similar size—by the piece. Worked stone was measured

---

[1] Both these terms occur in the fifteenth century. Kirby Muxloe Accounts, op. cit.

[2] Though it seems almost incredible, there is a record in 1355 (Pat. Rolls) of the purchase for Westminster of ' 20 cart loads ' of Egremont stone from a quarry near to Dunster. No doubt it was carted to the sea coast and so brought.

[3] For instance, the alabaster ' table ' (see p. 54) which was brought in 1367 from Nottingham to Windsor and took ten carts for seventeen days. Pat. Rolls, 41 Edw. III.

[4] It is also very probable that the development of vault ribs was suggested, at least in part, by a like difficulty in the matter of scaffolds and centerings. Some of the ribs were set with a very simple turning-piece which could be adjusted for varying spaces.

[5] Beer in Devonshire; still famous for its stone.

[6] *Carratata.* A Yorkshire local term *tuntight* equalled about 40 feet cube. *Damlade* was another local term of weight.

by the foot superficial or by linear dimensions, and also by the piece, *ad tascam*.

The general waste stone or spoil was called *les rubbez* or some such term ; and it was often used up for in-fillings of thick walls and piers or rough and unimportant building work.

Cyment was used for bedding and jointing and also lime and mortar; the lime was burned in a *calcifornium* or *rogus* or a *lymeputt* [1] and in use *drawkyng* or *slecking* proceeded just as it is done to-day. [2]

They used concrete, *attractum* or *attraytum* for various purposes, but particularly for wall in-fillings ; and the water required for their work was kept at hand in large vats or tubs called *fattez*.

The scaffolding, *scaphalda*, had *standardes* or vertical poles which were in the earlier times often of rough trees, [3] but in later of round or squared timber (called *quarters*). As the work went up they left holes for the putlogs, *staykfaldhollis* or *grapa*, and a number of these were referred to as *columbaria*. The jointings of the various poles of a scaffold were made with ropes called *twichyngropes* and with withes, and they were drawn tight with wedges called *warokkes*. For the flooring of scaffolds they used planks, and *flekes* or hurdles for protecting the edges. [4] An illustration [5] of fifteenth-century date shows a scaffold borne on brackets at a high level on which a man works. Cradles, *credills*, or swinging scaffolds [6] were also used occasionally for repair work. They apparently used gloves when doing scaffold work. [7]

Scaffoldings and tackle of all sorts were sometimes provided by the building owner, and at others were found under agreement by the master-mason. For building the monks' dormitory at Durham, *c.* 1401, ' scaffaldes, seyntrees, and flekes ' are mentioned in the indenture. In other instances and more frequently, references are found to them in various building accounts and contracts.

[1] Lime burning consumed an immense amount of wood fuel ; it was not until towards the end of the thirteenth century that mineral coal was adopted. There are many records of the grant of trees from forests for lime burning. The kilns, *torale*, were built of brick in the thirteenth century. York Fabric Rolls include the details of cost of one built in 1400, in which clay appears to have been used in place of mortar.

[2] Villard de Honnecourt gave a mixture for mortar—' lime and pagan brick and linseed oil '—and averred it to be of excellent quality.

[3] ' 15 great poplar trees bought for scaffolds, 11s. 6¼d.' Exeter *Fabric Rolls*, 1325.

[4] For the making of these hurdles they used rods, cf., ' . . . for cutting rods . . . for making hyrdulles therefrom for scafoldyng . . .' Kirby Muxloe Accounts, 1480-4, op. cit.   [5] Cott. MS. Aug. V. f. 51.

[6] These are mentioned in the *Fabric Rolls*, York, and at Windsor, and elsewhere.

[7] This may be particularly noted in the *Fabric Rolls* of Exeter.

Besides the apprentices of their trade the masons had labourers ;
bayardours, barrow-men who used one or other of the two forms of
barrows, *bering-barwes* having no wheel and requiring two men to
bear them, one in front and the other behind, and wheel-barrows,
civeria rotalis of the ordinary type. The edges of the wheels, *quheles*,
were either banded with iron strips called *strakes* secured with
strake-nails or had nails, *clutia*, only, the large heads of which
resisted the wear on the wooden rims, *quheill-ryms*.[1]

Bricklayers' work and the use of bricks for general walling is of
very much later date than that of masonry; the term does not
appear before A. D. 1450. Previously, in Roman times and thereafter, bricks were called tiles and were more like such in form ;
waltyles or *walteles* were often mentioned, but they were thin, 1½ in.
to 2 in. in thickness and of large superficial area, and they were used
more for bonding purposes than for direct building, but after
Elizabethan times bricks came into common use and all building
accounts are full of details concerning their use and manufacture.
There were ' great brickes ', 12 in. long, 6 in. wide, and 3 in. thick,
and ' statute bricks ', 9 in. long, by 4½ in. wide, and 2½ in. thick,
exactly the measure of modern standard bricks save that the latter
are usually ½ in. thicker.

The making and burning of bricks in kilns was a matter of
great controversy ; the continuous fumes from the kilns were
held to be prejudicial to the health of the community, and
a great deal of opposition was set up. Wood was the fuel in
the earlier times, but coal was adopted in the later.

In 1437 William Weysy ' brickmaker', the King's serjeant, was
appointed ' to search for earth suitable for making tiles, *tegulae*,
called " brike " and to arrange with the landowner to dig such
earth ' ; he was also to take coal, firewood, and other necessaries for
making such ' brike ', and all this and other duties were imposed on
him in respect of the King's manors at Shene and elsewhere.

Paventyle are frequently mentioned in earlier periods, and as the
name indicates were used for pavings,[2] and the layer was called
the *paviour*.

Mediaeval paving tiles, *paventyl*, are very much later in date
than those used for roofing. There were many well-known centres
whence they were obtained. They were made from a quite plain
sort to such as were decorated with considerable elaboration—

---

[1] Cart wheels were also so protected sometimes.

[2] Sometimes marble is mentioned for this purpose : ' Pro 1040 pedibus
de petra marmorea pro pavimento claustri 14*l*. 1*s*. 8*d*.' **Exeter** *Fabric Rolls.*

coloured, glazed, and incised white or tinted designs were employed. Beautiful examples came from Chertsey, others from Great Malvern and from Repton, Droitwich, and other places. In most cases these tileries appear to have been of monastic connexion, each of the above mentioned being connected with the religious house of the place. Such tiles being chiefly used in ecclesiastical work, their manufacture practically ended as the Reformation period drew near—the demand declined and the interest of the producers waned. In size they were generally about 5 in. square, though both larger and smaller examples are frequently found. Sometimes they were made in sets up to as many as sixteen or more to form a large design, and they often bore inscriptions, armorial bearings, and other enrichments.

The only term of measurement particularly applied to pavings is the *toise*, which was said to be 7½ ft. in length by the width of the ' foot of St. Paul '.[1]

Tiler's roofing work was a later industry, though not so late as that of the bricklayer.[2] As he depended on a burnt clay product he had to meet nearly the same sort of opposition in manufacturing as the latter, but when stone shingles were unobtainable the only fireproof roof was one of tile, and being demanded by Statute, must needs, therefore, be supplied.

In some districts, however, slates, *sclats*, usually of some laminated stone and of considerable thickness, were used. The Abingdon Accounts, 1404–5, mentions these and the *sclatpynnes* with which they were fixed on to the timbers of the roofs.[3]

Tiles for roofing purposes did not come into use before the thirteenth century and not often in its earlier years. Regulations in London, after the fire in 1212, required that roofs should be covered henceforward with tiles, for it was chiefly to the thatched roofs and those covered with wood shingles that the spread of the fire was attributed. This sort of legislation continued, but only slowly did it have effect.[4] In 1313 Queen Margaret proceeded to

---

[1] *Liber Albus*, London. *Toise*, Old French, was about 6 ft. 4 in.

[2] Sales of tiles are recorded in 1259 and 1275. In 1318 the bailiff of Naccott tile kilns (forming part of the royal manor of Wye) returned sales of 52,000 tiles at 3s. 3d. per thousand.

[3] *Accounts of Abingdon*, Camden Society, 1892, p. 76. In a later account 2,000 were bought for xs. viijd., *cum cariagio* (1436). These and stone shingles were often laid in moss, hence ' mossing ' a roof often occurs as an item of expense in accounts.

[4] Even in 1302 thatch was apparently still preferred, for one Thomas Batt entered into an agreement with the Mayor of London to indemnify all who might sustain damage if his thatched houses caught fire before he had got them tiled. London Letter Book C, fol. lxv.

re-roof certain of her houses with ' slates of stone and earthen tiles ' in lieu of oak shingles, *scindulae.*

In 1350, 24 Edw. III, enactments were made to control excess in charges and wages in many trades and amongst others by the tilers who strove to profit by the urgency of building affairs ; they were to have 5½*d.* a day in summer and 1*d.* less in winter, when the days were shorter. Tiles were to be charged at 5*s.* a thousand ' at the highest ',[1] but in 1350 in the London Bridge Stores tiles are rated at 8*s.* per thousand.[2]

After the ' tempest of wind which has of late unhappily occurred in divers parts of our realm ', Edward III, in A. D. 1362, issued a royal Order as to roofing materials and tilers' wages because, as it says, they were being charged ' at a much higher price than heretofore'. It directs that the older rates shall be retained, and threatens fine and imprisonment to those who fail to comply.[3]

Tiles, like bricks, were of regulation sizes as fixed by statute, and these sizes were approximately the same as of the modern tile. They made the sundry appurtenant tiles necessary for ridges and gutters of roofing work and also tiles for corners ; and all tiles were priced by statute nor could they be sold at other figures.

As to the method of making tiles the accounts of a large tile works in Kent, which extend from 1330 to 1380, give many interesting particulars.[4] The earth was dug in the autumn, allowed to lie during the winter and made up in the spring—exactly as the modern tile is produced. They were hand-made of course; no suggestion occurs anywhere of a pressed tile or brick.

The oldest trade in building concerns was that of the carpenter. This trade has ever been the dominant one in all such procedures, and by the time the mediaeval period was reached the carpenter had become a man of considerable proficiency, and upon him rested large responsibility in every building enterprise. He provided the carts, *carrectae*, for bringing the stones and other materials to the work, he made the barrows, found the timber for the scaffolding and erected it and the hoisting tackle ; he made the centres, *syntres* or *cintra* for the arches and the vault ribs and prepared the boards for setting-out the work and the moulds. He also made and erected all the timberings of the structure, framed its wall-pieces and its roofs and covered them in with boardings.

The records all along the times are full of detail as to the carpenter

---

[1] London Letter Book F, fol. clxxxi.
[2] Riley, *Memorials of London*, p. 262.　　　　[3] Ibid., p. 308.
[4] See Salzman's *English Industries* for quotations, and also other very interesting details. These tileries belonged to Battle Abbey.

and his work. He was generally known as the *carpentarius* but occasionally the term *domifex* ('maker of houses') is found. The material of his trade was often described as *meremium* (of which there are many orthographies) and, though that term was also employed to describe general building materials and even waste stuff of all sorts, it usually implied timber.

Axes, *dolabrum* a broad axe and *securis* the ordinary one, and the adze, *addice* or *ascia*, with the saw, were the principal tools. There were various kinds of saws: the *whip-sawe* for cutting boards and timbers of length; it was a narrow-bladed tool set in a frame and worked by two men, one below and the other above, the log being set over a pit or raised to a sufficient height on a pair of trestles. Then there was a cross-cut saw, called a *twhert* or *twortsawe*, and a smaller and wider bladed saw called a *serra* or *handsegh*; this latter usually had a curved scimitar-like cutting edge on which the teeth were cut. *Sarratio* was the term for general sawing and particularly of boards; *rendbord* was riven stuff generally used for roofs and laid across the rafters to receive the tiling or other covering; *sarking bords* were also used and *scindulae* or shingles of wood were frequently employed for the outer coverings.

They had chisels, *celtae*, gouges, an ordinary *goug* and a *thykstyll-goug*; this latter may possibly have been of adze form with a hollow gouge-shaped blade. There was also a tool called a *dryvelle* for hollow cuttings and their rebating was very much like that of to-day and had a similar name, *rabytyng*. Hatchets, *hachis* or *hakys*, were used of various sorts, and an axe called a *dolabrum*. The carpenter's plane, *planetorium* or *leviga*, was very much like the modern tool, having a blade fixed with a wedge in a wooden block which had a handle on the top. His brace or *wymbyll*, with its chest-rest and bits was also very modern in design, but the term *wymbyll* was also applied to an auger and that tool was sometimes turned by a cross-form head or handle; it was also called a *tarrera*. *Forpices* were pincers; a *mitrum* was a kind of set-square for making mitred joints; a *nail-percell* bit was for nail holes and was probably used in a brace and they had also a *spirula* or gimlet and another tool of the same sort called a *percours*. Pipe boring was done with a *terebellum* or *furfurculam*. They also used a lathe for turned work.[1]

Another kind of axe was named a *thixill*, but what its special purpose was is not clear, but the broad axe was used in preparing house-frames, *dolati*.

[1] A lathe and a *lathyre* and 'two old lathes' are mentioned in London Letter Book D, fol. xcix, 3 Edw. III, inventory of a cooper's shop. There is evidence also of the use of a lathe for stone turning.

The mediaeval builder apparently had appliances for operations which seem quite modern. Hormanus in his *Vulgaria* (1519) says that they moved a house bodily. He refers to the use of *trochs* and *slyddis*, and says that it was 'done with the myght of men and oxen'. It has been suggested that this was not the first or the only case of such enterprising effort,[1] indeed a well-framed timber-built house would move easily enough on properly prepared 'slides', well greased as no doubt they would have been.

At the beginning of the mediaeval period, say the tenth century, timber was very freely used for structural works, and in many cases wholly so. One of the earliest, if not the earliest example (though much restored) is that of the wall of the church at Greenstead (Essex). Here the timber wall-work is built solid of split adze-hewn trunks set close together with their flat faces turned inwards. But even in these early days timber was not generally used for church work, and when the Domesday Surveyors made their perambulations they recorded a 'church of wood' when they found one.[2]

As the centuries passed on, timber was employed in a more and more constructive manner and with the advent of stone, and later of brick for walling, it largely disappeared for external frame works, —it is not, however, necessary to discuss the matter further here.

Of the sorts of timber used, home-grown oak was by very far the most usual, and it was used for every kind of building purpose. Other timbers were used, but more sparingly—chestnut, for example, for roof work—a wood rather difficult to distinguish when old, as it looks much like oak.

Harrison, in his *Description of England*, says, ' in early times sallow, willow, plum-tree, hardbeam, and elm were used as well as oak but now (1587) all these are rejected and nothing but oak any whit regarded.'

Certain timber, oak and fir, was imported from the Scandinavian peninsula—such stuff was generally termed *bordi Estrenses*, or *Estriche-borde*, or *Eastland* boards and came from Norway.[3] Fir was imported and used at Windsor Castle [4] in 1234 and at Winchester in 1252.[5] Occasionally such terms as *firsperres* or *furdelles* are used, evidently referring to fir timbers for roofs or floors, and *deals*, a term

[1] Stowe, *Survey*, op. cit., refers to such an operation, bk. 2, p. 17.

[2] Stone was first introduced into English use by Bennet, a monk, in the year 670, and was chiefly used for churches and bridges. J. Harland, *House and Farm Accounts*, 1856, Chetham Society.

[3] *Rigal* (Riga) boards are referred to in the Exeter *Fabric Rolls* at the beginning of the fifteenth century, also *rigalds* in the *York Rolls*.

[4] Hope, *Windsor Castle*.   [5] Liberate Rolls, 37 Hen. III.

still in use to-day. *Quarters* are mentioned, and these timbers are much of the size called *quarterings* to-day, viz. 4 in. × 2 in. or 4 in. × 4 in. ; they were used in partitions.

In the later periods very strict regulations were laid down as to the sizes and qualities of timbers. The Carpenters' Company, which dates from before 1270, had very extensive powers of search, inspection, and approval or condemnation of the timber prepared for sale or for building use.[1]

Rafters were called *chevrons* or *sparrys* ; a large beam in a roof-framing or elsewhere in a building was called a *dormond* or *dormawnte-tre* because on it rested or ' slept ' other timbers of lesser bearing ; the great chimney beam was called the *mantil-tre*, and the term *tre* appears to have been applied to any large timber which was or approximated the size of a tree in the work.

Wainscot is a term still surviving but with only a very restricted meaning to-day. It originates in two Old Dutch words, *waeg*, a wall, and *schot*, a board or boarding. *Waynscowttes* (and like ortho-graphies) refer to wall-panellings or boardings of oak, but to-day it usually only means a skirting-board round a floor.

The general timber framing made for house work was called the *dolatus* or *framyd-dolatus*. The side pieces of a door, the *dorestothes* or *dorestuythes* and the term *stoothes* or *studys* was also applied to the posts of partitions which were to be lathed and plastered or covered with boardings. These and other mediaeval names and terms are still persistent in those of to-day.

The framed timbers were generally morticed and tenoned to-gether in a solid workmanlike manner, and the joints bored and pegged with substantial oak pegs. They also used bands, cramps, and other ironwork where special strength was required and had screws, *twystis* of sundry sizes though not of very good thread, being generally hand forged.

Some idea of the value of carpenters' materials and work when executed may be obtained from the Inventory of Stores connected with London Bridge in 1350.[2]

> ' timber for 14 shops, fully wrought and framed for immediate building. 36*l*.'
> ' 120 pieces of elm for piles [3] at 2*s*. the piece.   12*l*.'
> ' 57,000 *hertlathes*, value 4*s*. per thousand.'
> ' 30,000 saplathes, value 2*s*. per thousand.'
> ' divers boards of oak and of *estrichesborde*.'

---

[1] Jubb, *History of the Carpenters' Company.*
[2] London Letter Book F, fol. cxcv.
[3] The piles were strengthened with irons valued at 4*d*. per iron.

The wages of carpenters were practically the same as those already given of masons.[1]

There were very many sorts of nails, with names denoting the purposes for which they were used, from the largest of *spykyngs* down to the small *tynkyllnailes* or *tingilnails* which were probably much like modern tacks or sprigs.

The larger nails were forged by the smith on the anvil and the smaller sorts were formed in a die or matrix called a *nayle-tulle*. Some sorts of nails were named by fancy after their resemblance in shape to certain things, such as *flywinges* or *sparables* (sparrow-bills).

Of the more important of the other allied trades probably that of the plasterer, *daubator* comes first ; his work was called *dauberium* and consisted first of all in filling up the spaces between the timbers of house-framings. This he did by inserting lumps of clay, the lumps being called *cats*, to fill up the larger spaces and then he daubed the whole with plaster. The laths at first used were hazel twigs, *wandys* sprung into grooves in the timberings. In later times and for other plasterings than on frames they used *hert-laths*, i. e. heart-wood lath of oak, and *sap-lath*, made from the sapwood of the tree. They were riven with a tool called a *frower* and were nailed to the *dalbynstours* or posts of the partitionings. At one time their size was fixed by Statutory regulations, *temp.* Edward III, heart-lath were 1 in. wide and ½ in. thick.[2] Plaster-work on surfaces was also called *pargetting*, but the term usually implied some sort of surface decoration. To-day the term pargetting only refers to the rendering of the inside of flues with mortar.

The plasterer also *torched* the underside of roofs with mud and straw to fill the interstices and make it wind-proof, and he was at times therefore known as the *torchiator*.

The chief material of this trade was lime, and note has already been given of its production. They also used ' plaster of Paris ' : this material is merely calcined gypsum (sulphate of lime); when and how its quick-setting characteristic was discovered is not known. Gypsum was found in various places in England,[3] and in mediaeval

[1] Exeter Rolls, 1299, gives particulars such as ' i carpentarii cum garcione suo per 4 dies, 20*d*.' ' In stipendio Magistri Walteri carpentarii, 2*s*. 3*d*.' (for a week).

[2] An Ordinance of the sixteenth century said—' the lath shall conteyne in length v fote and in brede ii ynches & in thyckenes half a ynche of Assyse upon payne for every c lathe put on sale to the contrarye, ii*d*.' : very thick and heavy ! Beech lath were also used but less often than oak.

[3] It was also found at a place not far from Paris at a quite early date ; hence the term *plaster of Paris* which was made by calcining the stone.

times they quarried and burnt it as early as the beginning of the thirteenth century or even the latter part of the twelfth. *Plastre de Nower* and *plaster de Corf* are also mentioned, both being calcined gypsum found in those places in the south of England. This plaster was used at times for building mortar, but could never have been so good as the calcined calcium carbonate.

Another important trade was that of the plumber, the *plumbarius* (or as one record has it, the *blumbarius*![1]); lead-mining is of very ancient origin in England, and mines existed in various places.

The use of lead dates back far before the mediaeval period, and throughout its use is frequent and the records have many mentions concerning its mining, smelting, and general use and control.[2] For building purposes cast sheet was one of the chief forms of its use; these sheets or pieces, never so large in area as the modern sheets, were very heavy, as much as 14 lb. per foot super, and were in use for purposes for which modern practise considers 5 lb. a sufficient and 7 lb. a liberal weight.

Lead pipe-work was also carried out by the mediaeval plumber, and he used ' little cunditts or spouts of brasse with . . . cockes of brasse '.[3] Tin was also used—' cundites of clene tyn '.

Lead was used for coffins from a very early date and throughout the mediaeval period, and for cisterns, fonts, and sundry forms of ornamental cast work, sometimes even for the small paterae attached to late wooden roofs or ceilings and which were painted or gilded.

In 1365 the Ordinances of Plumbers [4] indicates the effort of the trade to obtain fair and satisfactory conditions by statutory obligation. It required proper trade education and that work should be done ' well and lawfully '—it fixed the rates of payments: ½d. for working a clove [5] of lead in gutters or roofs; in conduits and more difficult work, 1d. was to be paid.[6] There were also many other

---

[1] 'Stipendio blumbarii (*sic*) . . . 43s. 4d.' *Compotus Roll*, Worcester, vol. ii, p. 9.

[2] See Salzman's *Industries*, pp. 41–68, giving a full and interesting account of lead-mining and industry.

[3] *Durham Rites*, p. 70. This *brasse* may have been what is known as *latten*, an amalgam very much like brass. See also *Archaeologia*, vol. xxi, pp. 261 and 262. 'Lavoures of latun ' are mentioned in *Piers Ploughman's Crede*; he also mentions the use of tin.

In 1418 a new brass cock for St. Peter's fountain at Exeter cost 6s. 8d. *Fabric Rolls*.

[4] London Letter Book E, fol. cxlix.

[5] A *clove* was about 14 lb. and as sheet lead was often that weight to the foot superficial it would indicate only a small area of metal laid.

[6] At Exeter the master-plumber had 6d. and his servant 5d. a day. *Fabric Rolls*, 1424.

regulations of a like salutary character and penalties enforceable in the breach thereof.

The smelting of lead was early recognized as a very injurious process. In 1371 there is record of a complaint to the Mayor of London [1] by the ' good folk of Candelwykstrete and of St. Clement's Lane in Estchepe ' that certain plumbers melt their solder ' to the great damage and peril of death of all who shall smell the smoke ' ; the complainants asked for and obtained an injunction if the plumbers did not raise the shaft of their furnace to a higher level so that the fumes might be better diffused.

The lead when smelted was cast into ingots (this being usually done at the mines) ready for the plumber to resmelt for the purpose of his sheets, &c., or for the refiner to extract the silver it contained. An interesting ingot was discovered at Kenilworth on the Abbey site, date *c.* 1535. It bears the stamp of Henry VIII's Commissioners,[2] and its weight is about 11 cwt. As it is a very late example it can scarcely be taken as a sure form of mediaeval ingot casting ; the molten metal was evidently cast in earth.

Tela plumbi meant literally a lead tile, but in practice it referred to a sheet of cast lead of an ordinary workable size ready for a roof, whereto it was fixed with *leydnayles*, i. e. nails dipped into molten lead (or sometimes tin-dipped). To dress the edges of such sheets and smooth their surfaces there were lead planes or *hukschaves*, hook-shaves. The joints were burned with a *burnyngyrynnys*, and *knotts* or joints were formed in pipe-work with the same tool. For this and other jointing purposes they had *sowdre* and *soudynghirnes* and used rosin as a flux.

The weights used for dealings in lead were the *carretata* cart load,[3] equal to 24 *fotinels* (each 70 lb. or 14 *cuts* [4] of 5 lb.) A *kintale* or *quintale* was also a weight for metals ; it varied from 96 to 120 lb.

The smith, *faber*, had a forge with bellows, *suffleti*, and *twyrne* or blast-pipe. His great hammer was called a *foyrhammer*, and he had a *hewyryn*, a chisel held on a hazel twig, for cutting rods, &c., and other necessary tools, and did his *ffilyng* with files which were cut

---

[1] Letter Book G, fol. cclxxiii.

[2] *Birmingham Archaeol. Soc. Trans.*, vol. xlvii, p. 93, gives a description and illustration.

[3] Approximating 15 cwt. modern weight. The *carretata* seems a very vague measure. It was also used for other items than lead. It varied, as did many weights and measures, according to the district. In London at one period the *carretata* equalled 2,000 lb., i. e. approached the modern ton, and later it went up to as much as 2,430 lb.

[4] *Cuts* (not *cwts*), probably a cut off an ingot.

by the *vilhackere*. Steel, *asserum*, was bought in rod form, by the *faggot* of 120 lb.[1] Iron, *yryn*, was home found and smelted and refined on a *strynghearth*, and some was of foreign make, principally Spanish and imported. Iron was very dear in the mediaeval period, particularly in the earlier years—almost as dear as copper or brass, and steel was four times as costly.[2]

The smith repaired and sharpened the tools for other tradesmen, and he *layd* them with fresh steel as necessity demanded. Items ' for *battrynge* of the masons' tools ' are entered in accounts.

The name of *blaksmyth* is also to be found as early as the fifteenth century ; in an appointment cited in the Patent Rolls one was ' to take *blaksmythes* for certain works and purvey materials ' and other necessaries of his ' mistery '.[3]

Glass was little used in England until the thirteenth century and then almost exclusively in ecclesiastical buildings.[4] In the earlier periods screens of oiled linen, or frames filled in with sheets of horn were used to admit light, and wooden shutters for protection, indeed one at least of the purposes of clerestory passages in church walls was to allow access to the window shutterings.

Domestic glass, like wall panellings, was, so to speak, a tenant's fixture and was removable. Foreign-made glass was often put into English work in both early and late periods, and there are many notable examples of painted work of this sort. Glass was also made in England at an early date.[5]

Glass was measured by various standards: the *wey* being 5 lb. and the *hundred*, 24 *weys* ; a *table* (sixteenth century) consisted of 120 ft. superficial, this measure was also called a *long hundred* ; a *pondera* [6] was the same as a *wey*, and a *seam* 24 *weys*, and there-fore equalled a *hundred* ; a *stone* was also apparently the same

---

[1] A *burthen* of *gad* steel = 9 score or 180 lb. ; it also was called a faggot.

[2] Thorold Rogers, *Six Centuries of Work and Wages.*

[3] Pat. Rolls, 1496.

[4] Probably some glass was used at Canterbury in the new work after the 1174 fire. Salzman, op. cit., gives an eleventh century illustration (p. 191) showing glass-makers at work blowing glass from a furnace, taken from Schopper's Πανοπλία, 1568. Bede says it was introduced as early as 674 at Wearmouth, and it is recorded that in 709 the Bishop of York sent to France for glass to be used in windows previously closed with boards having holes in them for light.

[5] By 12 Edw. I the Abbot of Vale Royal was to have ' ferns in the forests . . . in order to make glass '. Close Rolls, 1284. It was evidently a well-known proceeding then, and the necessity for potash in its manufacture was also known.

[6] The term *pondus* referred to a weight of different amount with various materials ; of glass = 5 lb.

as a *wey*. A *krib* of cut glass equalled 100–150 ft. superficially; *sheiffes* of glass are also mentioned, and the terms a *poise*,[1] a *wave*, or *whisp*, or *loysp* are to be found.[2]

The *glassiers* cut, or rather cracked, their glass into rough shapes with a heated *grosser* or *croisure* with which they followed the lines of the design over which the glass was laid, being fixed down for the purpose with *clozyngnailes*; the final shapes were attained by nibbling away the glass edges with nippers. Diamonds do not appear to have been used until the seventeenth century.

The painter, *paintour*,[3] had size, *cole*, and oils and varnishes, *vervellum*, and the beer, *cerviscia*, which he used as a fixative for the whitening he laid over boards for designers to work upon, is also mentioned as one of the items of his affairs. White-washing, *dealbacio*, was a work which he seems to have shared with the plasterer, for the term *dealbator* may also mean a plasterer. Lime-whiting is very obviously referred to in the term *decalcare*, and *lambruscuram* often had a like meaning.[4]

In many of the trades work was done by the piece, *ad tascham*; at other times, and perhaps more often, it was done under the direction and oversight of a master, according to the rules of the guild to which he and the workmen belonged. But in post-Elizabethan times nearly all work was by contract, and indentures were the customary procedure.

§ 8. On Mediaeval Drawings

There is considerable question as to how the mediaeval master conveyed the ideas he had in mind to the actual worker. The most natural supposition is that he made use of drawings, but when search for these is made the results are very meagre, and there is much conflict of opinion about them. Some of the work he actually did by his own hand, but even for this he must needs set-out, and evidences of such procedure are naturally not often to be found, for the doing of the work obliterated them. Here and there some inscribed lines may yet be noted on such items as key-stones of vaults, where the general radiating lines of the ribs are marked out. There is a large inscribed plan on the floor of the Chapter House at

---

[1] About 5 lb., capable of ' glazing a window 2½ feet long and 1 foot wide '. *Memoriale of Henry*, Prior of Canterbury, fourteenth century.

[2] ' pro tribus whisps vitri '—Howden Roll, *temp.* Henry VIII.

[3] It is difficult to decide whether this was not the name of the painter of enrichments and frescoes on walls, more as the artist of to-day than the tradesman, but his ' mistery ' is referred to and that rather suggests the trade. A very free use was made of colour work on both stone and woodwork in mediaeval times.

[4] Sometimes this term referred to wainscot-work.

Wells, which is supposed to be the setting-out of the later buttress arches of the Crossing. In the crypt at York, on one of the capitals, there is part of the unfinished enrichment clearly set-out. Sketches, patterns, and models are known to have been used, but their existence to-day is very limited.

(*a*) Of actual working drawings a few examples may be cited ; (*b*) of sketches of mediaeval date there are also a few ; and (*c*) of pictorial scenes, some are to be found incidentally set in sundry manuscripts ; (*d*) besides these there are instances of models in stone or wood. Of each of these a few notes are appended below.

Probably the scarcity of these records is due to the fact that even as to-day not much store was set on such instruments of procedure when once the structure they set forth was completed ; indeed, if parchment had been used for drawings it was of such value that they were frequently cleaned off and the skins re-used, and *palimpsest* drawings evidencing this have been found.[1] Drawing materials were costly and rare—it took the skins of a whole flock of sheep to produce a book of any size. Then contemporary drawings of work in progress were often made in charcoal on large setting-out boards or on canvas, and charges for these materials occur from time to time in the records.[2] Such drawings could not be preserved, and the setting-out on the stones themselves was obliterated as they were worked.

There is, however, no question that serious drawing work was done. Evidence is clear as to this and as to the office wherein the drawings were made.

At Exeter in the *Fabric Rolls*, 1374–5, there is an entry,[3]

' Custos nove domus in Calendarhay vocate " trasyng hous ", 9*l*. 19*s*. 7½*d*.', evidencing a place for the making, i. e. tracing, drawings.

In the record at York [4] 1389, there is a mention of *tracynbordes* as being in the *loge*. In the Clerk of Work's Accompte, 1582, an

---

[1] Amongst others a thirteenth-century design possibly for some part of Rheims Cathedral, see Didron, *Annales Archéologiques*, vol. v.

[2] Ely Sacrist Rolls (first year of the building of the Octagon, 16 Edw. II) : ' bordis empt. pro moldis cementariorum faciendum '—' crombis ferreis pro moldis cementariorum.' In the painter's expenses (10 Edw. III) ' canevas et pergamena empt. pro moldis ' ; which seems to indicate that the drawings were made and then pricked through on to the stones.

At Westminster, when Master Thomas, the mason, went there to work on the new Chapel of St. Stephen, there is a record—' et intrasura super moldas operanti ', and also ' et tractanti super trasurum ' (4 Edw. III).

[3] See Oliver's *History of Exeter*, 1861.

[4] *Fabric Rolls.*

expense is entered ' for xj daies worke on the leades over the *tracinge hows*, etc., 10s. 8d.' The word *trasour* also occurs elsewhere— and all these refer to drawing work done within doors as apart from setting-out on stonework, &c.

(a) Dealing with the classes mentioned,[1] first as to working drawings. Of these there are very few indeed, and it is very doubtful if those which might be so termed were actually drawings made for the execution of work. For example, there is a ground-plan of the monastery at Canterbury ; this sketch was inserted in the illuminated Psalter of Eadwin ; its date is about the middle of the eleventh century.[2] It is a curious and crude drawing showing the buildings partly in plan and partly in elevation, and giving, at the same time, sundry enlarged details of doors and other items which the draughtsman's caprice dictated. It also shows the lines of the drains or water-courses, and gives such detail with these that it has been suggested that the purpose of the drawing was rather that of a drain plan than a builder's lay-out (see Plate I).

Another instance of planning of this sort, but much more carefully drawn, is that of the monastery of St. Gall[3] in Switzerland. Its date is much earlier, *c.* 829 ; it is a very complete and careful plan, drawn in red lines on a parchment, and though there is no attempt at scale, some figured dimensions are given, and the whole is annotated in detail by Eginhard (who may have been the architect) in Latin verse.

There are other examples of foreign drawings, some of fourteenth century date, of Cologne Cathedral,[4] of the tower of St. Stephen's, Vienna,[5] and of St. Maclou, Rouen.[6]

There are also the drawings of Sienna Cathedral and two elevations of that of Orvieto, the latter attributed to Lorenzo di Maitani of Sienna, *c.* 1310, when he was *capo-maestro* there. These are drawn in slight perspective and—

> ' are the nearest approach to working drawings to be found in the Middle Ages. . . . I doubt (says Sir Reginald Blomfield)

[1] A considerable list of drawings is given in the Architectural Publication Society's *Dictionary of Architecture*.

[2] The Psalter is now in the Library of Trinity College, Cambridge. A reproduction of the drawing is given in *Vetusta Monumenta*. To a certain extent the buildings it represents can be traced even to-day.

[3] The original is still preserved in the Library of the monastery. See *R.I.B.A. Trans.*, 1887.

[4] Shown in *Fac-simile der original Zeichnung*, Moller, Darmstadt, 1818.

[5] Illustrated in *Allgemeine Bauzeitung*, pl. 528, 1844.

[6] Enlart, op. cit., mentions twenty-two at Strasburg and many in Spain, though of later date.

PLATE I

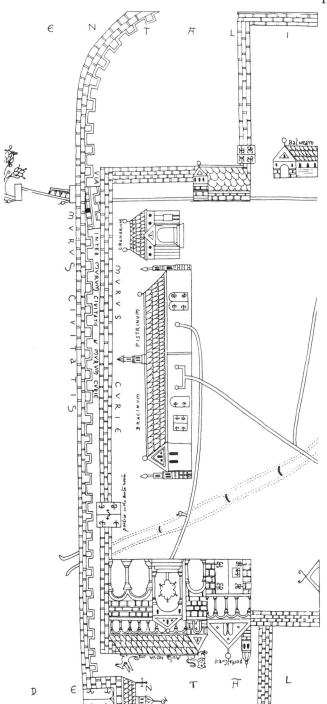

Plan of part of the precincts of Christ Church Priory, Canterbury (11th Cent.)

if they were made with that object or that the necessity for working drawings was seriously felt by the Gothic builders . . . if it came to carrying them (the drawings) out it is quite possible that little more than such rough indications as these would have been given to the builders, complete and well-founded reliance being placed on the traditional knowledge of the master mason . . . great architecture was essentially a builder's art . . . designers worked in the concrete and not in the abstract.'[1]

The same writer further adds:

' Even in the fifteenth century it is not to be supposed that a man like Sir Reginald Bray worked at a drawing board . . . when he had to deal with Henry VII's Chapel. . . . His share was to organize and administer and to decide on the general purpose and character of his building. The workman, with an immemorial tradition behind him, would have no difficulty in interpreting directions. . . . In the early days of Renaissance, introduced and run by scholars . . . it had to be explained down to its minutest detail to unlearned and ignorant men and thus architectural draughtmanship . . . became an absolute necessity.'[2]

In a book by Geoffrey de Monmouth (fourteenth century)[3] are some marginal sketches of towns, buildings, &c. Another drawing made on vellum, date 1421, is of the old steeple of St. Michael's, Cornhill.[4]

Examples of English drawings of the fifteenth-century date are more numerous. William of Worcester, in his *Itinerary*, made, or was given, a drawing of the door and arch mouldings of St. Stephen's, Bristol.[5] He also recorded the various names of the component mouldings of the groups; this also he was probably told.[6] He speaks also of the west door of St. Mary's, Redcliffe: ' The west Dore fretted yn the hede wyth grete Gentese[7] and smale, And

---

[1] *Architectural Drawing*, Sir Reginald Blomfield, p. 12 et seq.

[2] Blomfield, op. cit. He suggests that the informality, the habit of improvization, the irregularities and the neglect of symmetry may all be possibly attributed to the absence of drawings.

[3] Brit. Mus. Roy. MS. xiii. A 3 (see *Building News*, 4 Sept. 1868).

[4] See *Londina Illustrata*, Wilkinson, 1819.

[5] It has been suggested, and probably with accuracy, that William did not and could not make this drawing for himself, but that it was made for him by the master-mason on the work. The date both of work there and of his visit makes this quite within the verge of possibility.

[6] There are no less than twenty-four individual forms of moulds in the jamb of the door, and the names are given. William says : ' Thys ys the jame moold of the porche dore yn the north syde of the chyrche of Seynt Steuyn.' See *Itinerarium Willelme de Worcestre*, edited by Jacobus Nasmyth, A.M. S.A.S., Cambridge, 1782, p. 220.

[7] Cuspings.

fylled wyth entayle . . . rych wyth a Double moolde costley Dun and wrought.' In 1446 'draughts' on 'Eastland boards' were prepared before Sir William Sinclair set about building Roslyn Chapel.[1]

In the British Museum is a fifteenth-century drawing of the design for the tomb of Henry VI. It is a very careful piece of work, and drawn with a fine sepia-tinted line with fine ruled work and compass-drawn curved lines.[2]

Some drawings of King's College, Cambridge, exist.[3] One of these shows the north and east sides of the chapel in a poor sort of perspective. It is a peculiar drawing, partly coloured, and it exhibits some features of the building which are not now to be seen.[4] There is another drawing which shows a tower which was intended to be placed hard by the chapel. The lines are drawn in black, carefully ruled, and a tint of blue colour is washed over the building.

In the same collection there is a free-hand drawing of somewhat poor workmanship ; it is probably of later date than the others. There are also still later drawings showing very marked Italian influence in design.

The '*patren*' is mentioned in the covenant for the tomb of Henry VII in the chapel at Westminster;[5] a '*plotte*' and a '*picture*' are also referred to. A '*plat*', identified by his signature as approved by Henry VIII, for work at King's College, Cambridge, is mentioned in two indentures signed by the Wardens and the masons who contracted to do the work.[6]

In the contract (1439) for the Beauchamp Chapel at Warwick there is a reference to the '*patternes on paper*' and to the '*portraicture*', the latter possibly referring to the figures of the Earl and his wife which were executed by William Austen.[7]

By the time the sixteenth century is reached, the use of drawings had become very general and quite a number have been preserved ; many of these may be seen in Sir John Soane's Museum, London, chiefly by John Thorpe, a well-known architect of the time, who also prepared a *Sketch Book*.

(b) Of the second category there is practically only one example to cite, but that is quite an important one. It is the *Sketch Book* of Villard de Honnecourt.[8] This man was a French archi-

---

[1] See Britton, *Architectural Antiquities*.
[2] Brit. Mus. Cott. Coll. Aug. ii.   [3] Brit. Mus. Cott. Coll. Aug. i, vol. i.
[4] Mr. Papworth thinks that this drawing is of sixteenth-century date.
[5] This may have referred to a model.
[6] Britton's *Architectural Antiquities*, vol. ii.
[7] See Chatwin, *Monumental Effigies*, Birm. Archaeol. Trans. vol. xlvii, p. 62.
[8] *Album de Villard de Honnecourt*, Willis, 1859.

tect[1] of the thirteenth century; he was evidently a carefully trained man. He made drawings of the various buildings he visited, adding comments to his sketches of the points of interest he noted. He also made sketches or studies of figure subjects and ornamental detail of all sorts, and, furthermore, worked out sundry constructional and scientific problems including a curious scheme for perpetual motion. All these he set down in his *Sketch Book* with greatest care. The drawings are on vellum and were first made with a lead or silver point and afterwards gone over by hand with blackish ink; many lines were ruled and circles put in with compasses. A very curious feature about Villard's sketches was that he did not draw everything just as he saw it, but rather as he would have executed the work had he done it himself, and so much so, that in some instances it would be hard to recognize the work he portrayed were not the identifications made sure by his careful annotations.

Very few of his drawings would be useful for actual working, for in them elevation and perspective are often so mixed up together that it is difficult to determine exactly what is meant; it is improbable, however, that he intended them for anything more than general impressions of the things he had seen. Some of them are clear enough—plans, details of construction, and the like—but even these are not working drawings.

(c) Of the last category, pictorial sketches in manuscripts, there are quite a number and they are of a most interesting character. They occur somewhat erratically in connexion with all sorts of unlikely subjects, though chiefly in sacred works. In an eleventh-century manuscript, in the Cathedral Library at Durham, there is a curious sketch in pen-work, of the temple of Ezekiel, plans, elevations, &c., executed in the Romanesque manner, and as an illustration to the ' Prophecy of Ezekiel '.

These drawings are valuable because they give much contemporary detail on matters of building procedure, for there can be no question that the artist who used the costume and other items of his common daily experience, gave also the current practice in building operation as he saw it being done. And all such anachronisms may be gladly forgiven in that they record details of the times which might not otherwise have been readily known. Noah, for example, is shown in the Bedford *Book of Hours*, as a well-conditioned burgher of the

---

[1] Villard was certainly much more like a modern architect than any other of whom there is record ; he travelled a good deal in France, Germany, and elsewhere for the purposes of study.

fifteenth century, with the men working to his direction attired in trunk-hose and peaked caps; or Romulus is to be seen, in a Venetian manuscript, overlooking the workers on the city of Rome as they build a wall the like of which was never jumped across by his ill-fated brother Remus, but which bristles with Gothic towers and traceried gables.   Nor was this kind of representation confined to European artists, for there is a Persian manuscript [1] which shows building work going on at the palace of one of Bahrām Gūr's wives. The men are in native costume and are shown engaged in the operations of masonry: some work on the walls from a scaffold with its poles and ledgers, which they reach by a ladder of eight rungs; one man is carrying a piece of stone up the ladder, going up with his back towards it! On the other side a labourer is hoisting a basket of mortar or stones, and lower in the picture others may be seen carrying a basket on a bearing-barrow; several more workers are dressing stones with axes or mixing mortar.   It is curious to note that the mortar troughs or baskets and the procedures in working the stones are almost exactly the same as are shown in like drawings in English and Continental manuscripts.

Reference to the various Plates will show many of these building customs, and full notes are given with them.

There are one or two more illustrations of building procedures to be noted.   On one of the walls in the Lady Chapel at Winchester is a thirteenth-century fresco which depicts a building scene.   It appears to be concerned with the story related by Gregory of Tours which tells that the Emperor Constantine was once building a church to the honour of the Blessed Virgin, and that some of the columns which were brought for it were too heavy to raise.   The Virgin was said to have appeared and to tell the masons: ' Be not sad for I will show you in what manner you will be able to raise the columns ', and that is the operation depicted.   The Virgin, crowned, stands with a workman (probably the master-mason), who holds a large square and kneels before her.   In the rear of the scene are three children working a capstan which is fitted with four spokes and stands on a triangular base-frame.   The rope runs through a pulley at the ground level and thence upward over one suspended above, and then is fastened to a large beam which is being easily raised. The mason wears a large *gipciere* or purse, and an axe and an auger

---

[1] The Five Romances of Nizāmī, containing drawings attributed to Bihzād, the favourite artist of Bāhar.   The MSS. are on leaves of vellum and of fifteenth-century date; they may be seen in the British Museum.   The drawing here referred to is signed by the artist.

lie on the ground near at hand. In the rear is the outline of a church with windows.[1]

Besides the instances given there are a very few to be found in the glass of stained windows.[2]

(d) Then as to models or patterns. These without question were quite frequently used. Reference is often made to them in agreements, and some are shown on monuments and buildings. The model—probably a fairly complete one—of the tomb in the Chapel of Henry VII at Westminster [3] is referred to in the agreement with Torrigiano the mason or sculptor. Patterns of the work at the Beauchamp Chapel, Warwick, made in wood, are mentioned in the contract.

Models may also be found in connexion with work at various places on the Continent. Libergier's tomb slab (previously mentioned) shows one in the hand of the architect, and there are other instances elsewhere, for example, that of St. Maclou, Rouen ; [4] or in Italy when in 1418 the Florentine authorities offered a prize of 200 gold florins for the best *modellum sive designum* for the proposed dome of the cathedral, which was won by Brunelleschi.[5]

A few further pictorial illustrations may be found in the following manuscripts and other works noted below.[6]

1. Cottonian MSS. Claud. B. iv. Eleventh century. This shows a man fixing a piece of wood (illustrated in Green's *Short History of England*, vol. i, p. 164).
2. Harleian MSS. 603. Eleventh century. Here men are seen working on the walls of a town, some with hammers and chisels cutting stone and others setting them in the work (Green, op. cit., p. 173).
3. *MS. of Rabanus Maurus, pl. cxiii. Eleventh century. Shows men building off a scaffold, the standards of which are tree trunks whose branches have been lopped off, but with sufficient remaining to form forks on which the ledgers can rest.
4. Additional MSS. Brit. Mus. 10292. *c.* 1316. Workmen making an incised slab.[7]
5. Additional MSS. Brit. Mus. 10293. Fourteenth century. A

[1] Greg. Turon de Glor. Mart., c. 9 ; Baronius, *Annales*, vol. iii, anno. 324, c. 115.

[2] Thirteenth-century work; see Didron, *Annales*, ii. 143 and 242.

[3] Britton's *Architectural Antiquities*, vol. ii.

[4] This model was reported as found, see *Architectural Record*, Aug. 1907.

[5] C. Guesti, *La Cupola di Santa Maria del Fiore*, p. 15.

[6] Those marked with an asterisk may be seen in Salzman's *English Industries*, 1923.

[7] Nos. 4, 5, and 6 are reproduced in the *Archaeological Journal*, vol. i, p. 301 et seq.

building of stone with doors and windows is shown (see also Hudson Turner's *Architecture*, ii. 105).

6. Additional MSS. Brit. Mus. 10294. A picture of the same period and kind as the previous one.
7. Additional MSS. Brit. Mus. 35321. Fifteenth century. A small picture tablet showing the building of a circular tower with a scaffold, crane, &c., and a number of men at work.[1]
8. Additional MSS. Brit. Mus. 35321. A similar tablet showing the building of a town with workmen, scaffold, tools, &c.
9. *Cottonian MSS. Brit. Mus. Aug. A. f. 22. Fifteenth century. Men building a tower under the direction of a master-mason who is robed and does not work.
10. *Cottonian MSS. Brit. Mus. Aug. A. f. 51. Shows another castle-building scene and an unusual ' bracket ' scaffold.
11. *MS. *in Bib. de le Ville*, Geneva. Fifteenth century. Shows the building of a castle and specially the tilers at work on the roofs. In the foreground is a mason dressing a stone and a carpenter at work with a large axe on a long beam.
12. *L'Histoire de Charles Martel*, Brussels Royal Lib. Fifteenth century. Shows a church-building in progress. Various workmen dressing stone under a shed, others with bearing and wheel-barrows carrying it to the work : the barrow-men use shoulder straps to take the weight off their hands. Fixers are setting the blocks in the walls and have their mortar in small tub-like hods. Parts of the wall piers are protected with thatch pending procedure.
13. Wright. *Mediaeval Architecture*, in Brit. Archaeol. Assoc. Journal, vol. i, 1845. This shows, though badly drawn, two sepulchral effigies said to be of itinerant masons ; one holds a pair of compasses and the other a two-fold rule.[2]
14. *Analecta Eboracensia*, by C. Caine, 1897. Here is given an illustration reproduced from a MS., showing an early representation of the city of York. Taken from Bib. Reg. Brit. Mus. 13, A. iii, fol. 32, a fourteenth-century MS. by Geoffrey de Monmouth.
15. Lysons' *Cambridge*. Showing a picture of the tower of King's College.
16. *Die Cronica van der Hilliger Stat Coellen*, 1499, gives a print showing building work at Cologne. See frontispiece.

§ 9. NOTES ON THE ILLUSTRATIONS

The following Plates give examples of line drawings.

PLATE II, fig. i. *Building operations in the thirteenth century*.

The picture is from a Cottonian MS. in the British Museum. It is in two panels. The right contains three figures ; the central one is King Henry III giving instructions to the master of the works,

---

[1] Nos. 7 and 8 are from a French MS. The pictures are of considerable interest.   [2] See *supra*, p. 26, at Wooburn.

PLATE II

Fig. 1. King Henry III's building work (13th Cent.)

Fig. 2. 13th Century stone-masons

who is holding a very large pair of compasses in his left hand and is pointing, with his right, to the work which is shown in progress in the other panel. The third figure has no indication of office.

The right panel shows six workmen building an arcade, about which four others are variously employed ; one of the men is working with an axe on a square stone and another on a carved capital. Above the arcade the walling work has been raised four courses with large stones, and two men are laying other stones on the top. One man has a curious horse-shoe shaped plumb-bob rule.

There is a hoisting crane with a trunnion worked with spokes, and two men are hoisting a basket containing three stones. Access to the top of the crane is by a ladder of primitive type very much like a modern roof-plank, with cross pieces nailed to it for foot-hold.

fig. ii. *Stone-masons of the thirteenth century.*

This illustration is from a drawing in Didron's *Annales Archéologiques*, vol. ii, p. 143. It is a reproduction from a stained glass window.

It has two panels. The left shows a mason cutting a stone into shape with an axe. Behind him is another at work in building a tower, and he uses a long straight plummet.

The other panel also has two workers ; one works on a stone already partly cut for tracery-work, and uses an axe ; the other is working with a mallet and chisel.

Both panels are covered in with trefoiled heads under which are shown tools and patterns for stone moulding, &c. This illustration is particularly interesting on account of the display of these mould-pieces or templates, which are very much like those used by modern masons.

Plates III to VI are from illustrations in the *Sketch Book* of Villar (or Villiard) [1] de Honnecourt. The date of the book is in the first half of the thirteenth century, and its illustrations cover a wide area. He says ' *I have been in many lands . . . as this book shows* '. The book itself is now in the Imperial Library in Paris (S. G. *Latin* 1104). It is a small volume of thirty-three leaves of vellum, stitched into a thick rough leather cover, like a large pocket-book, but its present extent is probably much less than the original; many leaves appear to be missing (this inference is confirmed by the text). The drawings are made on both sides of the leaves. In the fifteenth century it is very certain there were more leaves, for there is a note

---

[1] *Vlardus de Hunecort* was probably his own spelling of his name. He probably built Vaucelles (*c.* 1230), and the choir of St. Quentin (*c.* 1250).

of that date at the end of the volume to say : ' *En ce livre a quarante et 1 feuillet. J. Mancel.'*

From this volume the following have been taken :

PLATE III.

(*a*) *The Towers of Laon Cathedral.*[1] These are, de Honnecourt says, 'the most beautiful that the world contains.' The drawing is merely a sketch, partly in elevation and partly in perspective of a crude sort. There is argument for the bulls he shows, but none for the human hand shown on the lower corner of the drawing (fig. i).

Another sheet gives a plan of this tower and some lengthy descriptions.

The modern drawing of the tower (fig. ii) is given for comparison's sake ; it also shows that subsequent alterations have removed some of the architectural details. There are no pyramidal roofs above the towers as in the sketch of Honnecourt, which also almost suggests a spire.

PLATE IV. ' These are the elevations of the Church of Rheims, and of the flat (aisle) walls within and without, &c., &c.' [2]

So the endorsement on the side reads, and speaks also of various details of the work.

The drawings exhibit one bay, externally and internally, of the nave of Rheims. The way in which they are set out is peculiarly modern in its method of drawing. The exterior is on the left and the interior on the right-hand side. Some compass work has been used for the arches and tracery, and other of the lines are partly ruled and partly hand drawing. The general proportions have unfortunately rather strayed from fact, but as an example of drawing work of the times, and indeed of Honnecourt's, it is excellent, and, moreover, it must have been made near about the time when the work was carried out, though it represents some details which apparently were never carried out, for no trace of them exists to-day —particularly the wall-arcade shown internally under the windows. It has been suggested that Honnecourt had access to original drawings which were not carried out.

PLATE V. The sketches are at Rheims Cathedral where Honnecourt evidently spent much time in study both of the exterior and the interior work ; he includes quite a number of sketches in his book. The one given here is of one of the apsidal chapels at the east end of the Cathedral. It is a very clear-cut drawing.[3]

---

[1] Plate xviii, Willis' edition, already cited (*verso* of the ninth leaf and *dorso* of the tenth).   [2] Plate lxi, ibid. (*verso* of the thirty-first leaf).
[3] Plate lx, ibid. (*recto* of the thirty-first leaf).

PLATE III

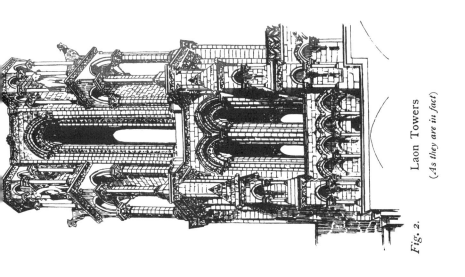

Laon Towers

(As they are in fact)

Fig. 2.

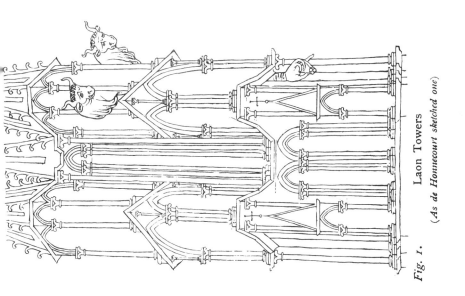

Laon Towers

(As de Honnecourt sketched one)

Fig. 1.

PLATE IV

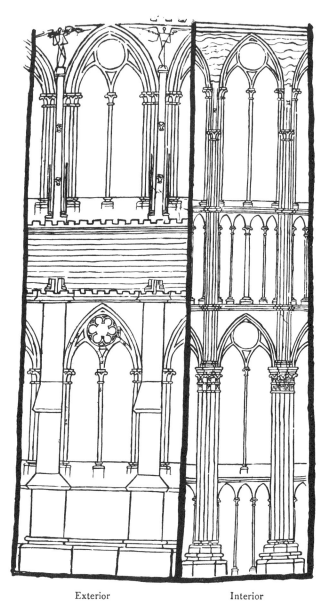

Exterior   Interior

Rheims Cathedral, Nave

PLATE V

Rheims Cathedral, Chapel

PLATE VI

Sundry constructive details, &c.

PLATE VI.   *Three sketches of constructional work.*[1]

i. (*Top, left side.*) This is a curious form of roof truss. ' Or poes veir i bon conble leger¹ por hierberger une chapele a volte' (*You see here a good light roof to cover a vaulted chapel*). It is a sort of hammer-beam framing without the wall brackets.

ii. (*Ditto, right side.*) ' Et si vos voles veir i bon conble legier a volte de fust prendes aluec gard ' (*And if you would see a good light roof for a wooden vault, look carefully at this*). It is evidently intended for a wagon-headed boarded roof-vault constructed high up in the truss framing.

iii. (*Bottom, left side.*) ' Vesci le carpenteri d'une fort acainte ' (*Here is the frame (or carpentery) of a strong pent-house roof*). *acainte* = a side-aisle.

iv. (*Ditto, right side.*) ' Vesci une esconce ' (*This is a sconce*).

The following Plates are taken from illuminated manuscripts in the British Museum.

PLATE VII.   *King Robert building and making war* (Harleian MS. 20 E ii, fol. 262).   French-English, fifteenth century, ' Chroniques de France ou de St. Denis.'

The manuscript distinctly says ' King ' Robert, but it doubtless means ' Duke '. It was written for Sir Thomas Thwaytes, Treasurer of Calais A. D. 1487, and was presented by him to Henry VII.

The king (or duke), wearing a crown, is shown discussing the building of a tower with the master-mason, who kneels before him, and is evidenced by his dress and the builder's square which he holds in his hand. Beyond him is a man working with a stone axe, and lying beside him, on a stone, is a pair of compasses and a square. On the ground is a plumb-rule with its bob. In the distance is the Duke's army.

It may be noted here that the master-mason is obviously the person in charge of the works and that he also works himself, for he holds one of the tools of his trade.

PLATE VIII.   *Building operations in various towns* (Harleian MS. 4376, fol. 150).   Venetian, late fifteenth century.

This very beautiful picture is divided into four panels, each of which shows building work proceeding in various places.

(*a*) (*Top, left side.*) This is a view of Venice, which according to

---

[1] Plate xxxiii, Willis, op. cit. (*verso* of the seventeenth leaf).

the manuscript was founded by the Trojans. The master-mason is shown, cap-in-hand, standing before some Trojan dignitary (possibly Priam, King of Troy). He holds in his hand a straight-edge, and by him is a mason working on a stone with a mallet and chisel and having a square lying on the stone he works. A second mason is working with a scabbling axe. Behind these are masons at work on three round towers, above one of which is a hoisting crane with a rope and wheel.

(*b*) (*Top, right side.*) The town is Cyambre, in Pavone (Italy). Here Helenus, son of Priam, is shown discussing some building procedures with one of his officials. The master-mason is approaching carrying his square, and near at hand are men at work using mallets and chisels and stone axes. In the rear are setters building the walls of the structure in hand.

(*c*) (*Bottom, left side.*) Here Dido of Carthage is viewing, with a lady and others, certain building operations in his city. Masons are at work with their tools in the fore-front of the picture.

(*d*) (*Bottom, right side.*) The last panel shows further building operations, and the statement on the picture is that the city is Rome and the principal figure Romulus. Before him is the master-mason bare-headed; he is carrying his straight-edge as a sort of evidence of office. The other workers shown are much as in the panels already described and their work is of the same sort of detail.

The leadership of the master-mason is evident in all these pictures.

PLATE IX. *Book of Hours* (Add. MS. 35313, fol. 34). Late fifteenth century.

The picture from this manuscript exhibits the building of an octagonal tower about which a scaffold is erected, having posts or standards, putlogs, ledgers and cross braces, exactly like a modern piece of scaffolding, and men are shown at work raising it a stage higher for the continuance of the building work. In the interior of the tower is a curious sort of derrick crane with its hoisting rope wound on a trunnion which is turned by spokes. At the end of the rope is a pair of quite modern caliper lifting grips.

In the distance is a thatched shed for the masons, in which a man is at work, having the stone on which he is employed raised on a bench or banker. In the yard is another worker, and a large pair of wheels for carrying heavy blocks of stone from the quarry.

In the head of the arch at the ground stage of the tower is the turning-centre still in position, and a man is passing under it bearing a basket-shaped hod or tray of mortar.

PLATE VII

'King' Robert's building work (15th Cent.)

(*Harleian MS.*)

PLATE VIII

Various building operations

(*Harleian MS.*)

PLATE IX

Building a tower (15th Cent.)

(*Additional MS.*)

PLATE X

Building a Church (15th Cent.)

(*Cottonian MS.*)

Plate XI

Building a House (15th Cent.)

(*Additional MS.*)

PLATE XII

Building the Tower of Babel

(*Additional MS.*)

PLATE XIII

Building the Ark (see page 94)

(*Additional MS.*)

PLATE X. From a French or Flemish MS. (Cottonian MS. Aug. A. x. fol. 416).

This is a particularly interesting picture, for it shows the use of temporary thatching to the roofs of the nave and porch of a church put on when the work was suspended during the inclement weather of the winter ; a similar thatched protection is also shown on portions of the unfinished walls.[1] The working is being watched by some royal person, for he wears a crown.

In the foreground are figures, in somewhat strange attitudes, bearing basket-hods of mortar, and another has a wheel-barrow with large round baskets on it.

It will be noted that the carved figures and ornaments appear to be completed on the side wall although the building is very far from being completed itself; also the buttress gablets have their enrichments carved as if finished off before setting in the work. This seems to bear out the record at St. Albans where carved work, &c., fell with the unfinished walls.[2] It is also curious that no scaffolding of any sort is shown.

PLATE XI. From a Flemish MS. (Add. MS. late fifteenth century, 19720, fol. 27).

The building in progress shown in the picture is apparently part of a house or hall, and the master-builder, who carries a huge plumb-bob, is attending a person of some importance. There is scaffolding about the building and men at work thereon. At the top of the wall is a gallow-like hoist with a rope raising a basket. One of the workmen has a pointed trowel and another an axe, and there is a basket of mortar. The hoisting is done with a crab with a trunnion but having no wheel.

In the centre of the picture is a carpenter at work with an adze and behind him two sawyers cutting a beam lengthwise with a whip-saw. Further down the picture are men at work digging a trench and another fixing the posts of a fence, using a long-handled mallet and other carpenter's tools.

PLATE XII. *Bedford Book of Hours* (Add. MS. 18850, fol. 17 b). Early fifteenth century. Flemish.

Building the Tower of Babel. This picture is taken from one of the most valuable manuscripts in the British Museum. It shows the two lower stages of a square tower and part of the third, with an

---

[1] This form of protection may also be noted in an illustration in *L'Histoire de Charles Martel*.　　　　　　　　[2] See p. 18.

external staircase winding round it. It is of a quite nondescript sort of architectural style.

The builders are at work on the upper part of the third stage and have a projecting scaffold. Two sets of hoisting tackle are shown, one from each stage; the lower has a winding crab with a wheel and two handles, and a double rope runs on the trunnion. The upper pulley turns on a pair of striding posts.

At the extreme top two heavenly messengers are shown troubling the workers, throwing some of them off the scaffold, and their stones, though the workers below are apparently quite oblivious of what is going on above.

In the foreground of the picture are various masons at work using compasses and squares and heavy scabbling axes, and other tools lie about on the ground including a broad dressing chisel. On the left side is a shed and a man mixing mortar and another shouldering a basket hod. Lower down are persons discussing the work, and on the right side is a man unloading stone from the panniers of a horse.

PLATE XIII. *The Building of the Ark.*

This illustration is also from the *Bedford Book of Hours* (fol. 15 in the MS.). It shows a huge wooden framework of squared timbers, with three floors and a ridge roof. Outside is a man, probably intended for the patriarch Noah, directing the work; he is pointing up to a worker who is nailing boards on to the roof, having a box of nails at hand for the purpose. At the other end of the roof-frame is a man driving in large wooden pegs to secure the framework together. Inside is a ladder extending through the upper floors, and on it a man carrying a beam on his shoulder. On the lowest floor are other workers, and at the end of the structure is one using a large tee-handled auger.

In front are various men at work: one with a plane, another with an auger, and a third using a long hand-saw with a scimitar-shaped blade. Sundry tools are lying on the ground, including a brace (of very modern form), a narrow bladed frame or whip-saw, a mallet, chisel, &c., and one worker is using a heavy-bladed axe. Sundry piles of cut timbers are shown, and beyond, in the landscape, are various buildings of importance and animals of sorts, apparently a beginning of the gathering for inclusion in the Ark when it is completed. Above, at the top of the picture, is a representation of God the Father encircled by a cloud.

This is quite the best illustration of carpentry work extant, and it provides much interesting detail.

APPENDIX I

Of the London Livery Companies it has been generally said :

' A distinctive feature of the London Gild in its fully developed form of a Livery Company was its Court . . . a court not merely in name. It had jurisdiction over its members, and even over outsiders who were engaged in the same trade. By its judgments unruly apprentices were whipped, journeymen on strike were imprisoned, and masters offending against trade regulations were fined. Members were forbidden to carry trade disputes before any other Court unless the court of their Company had first been appealed to in vain. This element of trade autonomy was a recognized part of the civic constitution and was supported if need arose by the authority of the Lord Mayor. . . .' [1]

Companies also existed in other towns, but often these for various reasons were compound Companies, for example, at Chester, the Wrights, Carpenters, Slaters, and Sawyers formed one Company, and the Joiners, Turners, and Carvers another ; [2] in Hull the Bricklayers, Tilers, Wallers, Plasterers, and Paviours joined in one ; [3] and they appear to have contained also the small contractor as well as independent masters and journeymen.

The Livery Companies, however, though they have practically nothing to do to-day with actual trade matters, perpetuate the existence of city trade guilds or confraternities. They were, as regards building matters, briefly as follows : [4]

1. *The Masons :*

By a code of laws apparently of 1356 date, workmen were divided into two classes—hewers and light masons or setters. Amongst others there were two special rules to be observed as to their craft : (i) no one should take work in the gross without giving security for its proper completion,[5] (ii) all apprentices should work in the presence of their master till proficient. The earliest record of a Charter to the Company is dated Sept. 17, 1677.

2. *The Carpenters :* [6]

There seem to be earlier records of the Carpenters than of the Masons. In 1271 two master-carpenters were charged in London

---

[1] *Gilds and Companies of London*, George Unwin, p. 28.

[2] Harl. MSS. 2054.

[3] Lambert, op. cit., p. 269. The Hull Bricklayers were very democratic— their ordinances were prefaced by the words : ' All men are by nature equal, made all by one workman of like mire.'

[4] See Hazlitt's *The Livery Companies of the City of London.*

[5] Regulations of Edward III, 1356, required him also to find ' six or four ancient men of his trade . . . to testify his . . .' skill and ability.

[6] See Jubb, *The Worshipful Co. of Carpenters*, for much interesting matter. Many details are given of the Company's powers of search for inferior material,

with certain surveys, and belonged no doubt to the Company to which Chaucer refers (*c.* 1388) as ' a greet fraternity '. Earlier in 1303, the name seems to hover between a craft and a patronymic— ' Wilhelmus filius Wilhelmi de Southwarke, carpenter '—' Philip le carpenter '—' Adam le carpenter ', and it was soon retained as a family surname.

3. *The Sawyers :*
An offshoot of the Carpenters, but failed to hold its position.

4. *The Joiners :*
This Company possessed Ordinances before 1309, under the approval of the City Authorities. The craft was quite distinct from the Carpenters and was limited to the making of doors, window-frames, wainscot, &c. They also made movable furniture. They too had rules on questions of materials, labour, and good behaviour.

5. *The Planers :*
Probably an offshoot of the Joiners but like the Sawyers also failed to hold its status.

6. *The Tylers and the Brickmakers :*
After the Fire of London in 1212 roofs of reeds or rushes were prohibited by Statute and were to be replaced with tiles, and though this was not immediately or completely done, later legislation continued to demand it.

Jack Straw of the 1381 Rebellion was a member of this Brotherhood, which was not incorporated with *the Bricklayers* until 1568. He was a master-tyler. In 1614 a petition was drawn up by these Companies praying ' that it may be enacted that the Asize of Bricke and Tyle and the measure of Lyme and sand may be observed in London . . . according to the Ordinances of the Master and Wardens of the Company '.

7. *The Plumbers :*
The most ancient regulations of the craft show that in the fourteenth century lead roofings to cathedrals, churches, &c., were becoming more common, and the quality of materials and expense necessitated careful safeguarding against dishonesty. Sheet lead then was heavy, about 14 lb. per square foot, and contained a considerable proportion of silver.

The Ordinances and By-Laws of the Company go back to *c.* 1365, and they refer to lawful weights, rates of labour, restraint of engrossers, purchase of old lead, stripping lead from roofs, &c. No member of the Company might carry out work alone if any fellow craftsman desired to share the labour and profits. Early in the seventeenth century other stringent rules were framed.

shortage of statutory scantling, and not a few of treatment for moral failures and general behaviour. In one case a badly built house was ordered to be rebuilt at the Contractor's expense.

8. *The Plaisterers or Pargettors :*

The most ancient document held by this Company is a Contract made by ' Adam le Plastrer ' citizen of London for plastering works for the Earl of Richmond, John de Bretagne. It is dated in 1317, and Adam agrees to find the Plaster of Paris and to complete the work within eight weeks on the security of all his goods.

The Company was very prominent from the time of Elizabeth and after. It appears to have had sundry disputes with the Tylers and Brickmakers on questions of trespass and collision, and in 1574 it fell foul of the Carpenters' Company on like interference matters.

9. *The Paviours :*

Stow (1598) thought it a ' company of antiquity ' but states that ' no Record doth testifie '. In the *Liber Albus* paviours were not entitled to charge more than 2*d.* for making seven and a half feet of pavement ' of the foot of St. Paul ' in breadth : this measure was called *a toise.*

10. *The Glaziers :*

This was not a large Company. It was at its zenith with the trade *temp.* Elizabeth.

It is not at all correct to claim that these, or practically any of the Livery Companies in their present-day existence, retain anything but traces of their early spirit and proposals. They are interesting relics of the past. The day of their real and vital purposes is entirely gone by and the ideals for which they rose into existence are not now in their keeping, if indeed, under modern competitive conditions, such exist at all. Neither they nor any form of *masonry* have purposes to serve or authority to exercise as they did in the days of mediaeval England. They are interesting survivals from which all trade practicalities have disappeared, leaving only their moral and beneficent elements—both of which qualities no doubt still exercise a sufficiently stimulating effect on those sections of the community that come within the sphere of their influence.

APPENDIX II

AUTHORITIES

Amongst the sources of information and authorities to which reference has been made for the purpose of this essay, the following may be quoted :

Abingdon Accounts. Camden Society, 1892.

Arnold, T. ' The Grete Sentens of Curs,' Wyclif, *Select English Works*, vol. i.

Archaeologia, Various papers in.

Antiquarian Reports. 1808.

Architectural Records. August 1907.

Architectural Publication Society. *Dictionary*, 7 vols. 1849–92.

Archaeological Journal. Vol. i., etc.

Audesley, W. J., and G. A. *Dictionary*, 1878.

Anselm, *Itinerary of*.

Blomfield, Sir Reginald. *Address* to the Birm. and Mid. Institute, 1924.
—— *Architectural Drawing.*
Bond, Francis. *Gothic Architecture*, pref. x., 1906.
—— *English Church Architecture.*
Brown, Baldwin, Prof. *Arts in Early England*, vol. i., 1903.
Browne, J. *History of York.*, 1847.
Britton, John. *Architectural Antiquities*, 5 vols., 1807–35.
Bell, W. G. *Great Fire of London*, 1920.
British Archaeological Association. *Congress at Winchester*, 1845.
Building News. Sept. 1868 and 1913–14.
Bedford Book of Hours, Add. MSS. British Museum.
Baronius. *Annales Ecclesiastici*, vol. iii, 1738.
Coulton, G. C. *Five Centuries of Religion*, vol. i, 1923.
Certain, E. *Miracles de S. Benoit*, Soc. de l'histoire de France.
Condor, E. *The hole crafte & Fellowship of Masons*, 1894.
Cottonian MSS, and other MSS, British Museum.
Close Rolls, Calendars of, 30 vols.
Cunningham W. *Mason Craft in England*, Address to Inter. Hist. Congress,
    1913.
Comité Historique des Arts, vol. i, 1843.
Caine, C. *Analecta Eboracensia*, 1897.
Davis, H. W. C. *England under the Normans and Angevins*, 1904.
Dodsworth, W. *Salisbury Cathedral*, 1814.
Dugdale, Sir William. *Monasticon Anglicanum*, 1817–30.
—— *Warwickshire*, 1730.
Durham Rites, Surtees Society.
Durham Account Rolls, Surtees Society.
Didron, A. N. *Annales Archéologiques*, vols. i and ii.
Enlart, C. *Manuel d'Archéologie française*, 3 vols. 1902–16.
Exeter Fabric Rolls.
Elyot, Sir Thomas. *Dictionary*, 1538.
Ferrey. 'English Mediaeval Architects,' Sessional Paper, *R.I.B.A. Trans.*,
    1865.
Funck-Bretano. *The Middle Ages*, Nat. Hist. of France Series, 1922.
Gardiner. *Guide to English Architecture*, 1922.
Guilhermy. *La Sainte Chapelle*, Paris, 1867.
Green, J. R. *Short History of England*, vol. i.   (Illustrated Edition.)
Historia Eliensis.
Hope, W., St. John. *Windsor Castle*, 1913.
Hudson Turner. *Domestic Architecture of the Middle Ages.*
Hoare, E. N. *History of Wiltshire.*
Hazlitt, W. *The Livery Companies of London.*
Harleian Charters, British Museum.
Halliwell, J. O. *Early History of Freemasonry.*
Hamilton Thompson, Prof. 'Accounts of Kirby Muxloe Castle', *Leics. Archaeo-
    logical Society Trans.*, 1923.
Hormanus, William. *Vulgaria*, 1519.
Issue Rolls, Calendar of.
Lanfranc, *Itinerary of.*
—— *Opera Omnia*, 1648.
Lambert. *Two Thousand Years of Gild Life*, 1891.

Lethaby, Prof. W. R. *Westminster Abbey.*
—— *Architecture.*
—— *Mediaeval Art,* 1912.
—— ' Education in Building,' Sessional Paper, *R.I.B.A. Trans.,* 1901.
London Letter Books.
Leland, *Itinerary of.*
Lysons, D. and S. *Magna Britannia,* Cambridge.
Martel, Charles, *L'Histoire de.*
Merzario, Prof. *Maestri Comacini,* vol. i.
Morter. *Recueil des Textes.*
Nichols, John. *Collection of Royal Wills,* 1780.
Nasmyth, Jacobus. *Itinerarium Willelmi de Worcestre,* 1782.
Nizami, ' The Five Romances of,' MS. British Museum.
Oliver, Archdeacon. *History of Exeter Cathedral,* 1861.
Power, Cyril E. *Lectures to the Goldsmiths' Company,* 1907.
Porter, Kingsley. *Mediaeval Architecture,* 1922.
Prior, E. S. ' Basis of English Gothic Architecture,' Paper to the Architectural Association, 1901.
Papworth, W. ' The Building Superintendents of the Middle Ages,' *R.I.B.A. Trans.,* Sessional Papers, 1861 and 1887.
Pipe Rolls, Calendars of.
Patent Rolls, Calendars of, 56 vols.
Quarterly Review. ' State of English Architecture,' April 1872.
Riley, H. T. *Memorials of London, Thirteenth to Fifteenth Centuries,* 1868.
—— *Liber Albus,* 1681 (ed. by Riley).
Ravenscroft, W. *Notes on the Comacine Masters,* Nat. Masonic Research Soc.
Rymer. *Fœdera.*
Raine, James. *Catterick Church.*
—— *York Fabric Rolls,* Surtees Society, 1858.
Royal Historical Society. *Transactions,* vol. vii (N.S.).
Simpson, Prof. *History of Architecture,* 1922.
Springer, Dr. Anton. *De Artificibus Monachis et Laicis Medii Aevi,* 1861.
Smith, J. T. *Antiquities of Westminster,* 1807.
Stubbs, William, D.D. *Chronica Gervasii,* Rolls Series, 1879.
Salzman, L. F. *English Industries of the Middle Ages,* 1924.
Traill, H. D. and Mann, J. S. *Social England,* 1901.
Unwin, George. *The Gilds and Companies of London.*
Vetusta Monumenta, 1789, etc.
Vale Royal, *Ledger Book of,* Lancs. and Cheshire Record Society.
Viollet-le-Duc. *Essays.*
—— *Dictionaire,* vol. i.
Watkins, W. ' St. Mary's Guild, Lincoln,' *R.I.B.A. Trans,* 1913 and 1914.
Willis, Robert. *History of Canterbury Cathedral,* 1845.
—— *Album de Villard de Honnecort,* 1859.
—— ' Nomenclature,' *Cambridge Antiquarian Society Trans.,* vol. i, 1840.
Wilkinson, R. *Londina Illustrata,* 1819.
Wright, T. ' Mediaeval Architecture,' *British Archaeological Journal,* vol. i.
York Fabric Rolls. Surtees Society, 1859.

(And other writers, and as mentioned in the foot-notes.)

FURTHER NOTES ON
THE
MEDIAEVAL BUILDER

BY

FRANCIS B. ANDREWS

Further Notes on the Mediaeval Builder

Communicated by FRANCIS B. ANDREWS, F.S.A., F.R.HIST.S.

THERE is so much more that might be said about the Mediaeval Builder and his work that it is a little difficult to select the most useful. It may, however, serve present purposes if the much-debated question of *style* development be a little further considered. It is a question inextricably connected with the master-mason and his work, and not even now has it been dealt with in a manner which fully satisfies critical opinion.

The facts regarding these *styles*—popularly so called—are well enough known; their executive sequence and the universality of their *motif* are undeniable and, despite whatever local variations may be noted, they are in general terms as unanimous in design as they are widespread throughout the kingdom. It was indeed with some show of reason that earlier writers on architectural history thought it right to parcel off the more pronounced examples and call them *styles*, but how these *styles* came to be, or by what means one followed another, or whether there was any sort of evolution in their sequence, they did not attempt to determine. Nor do any misgivings appear to have been held by them on the then current idea that their design and even their actual execution were to be attributed to the monks.

To-day, however, pertinent questions are being asked on all these points and they must needs be met with reasoned replies. There are those who are satisfied that the differences between the work of one period and another—the style developments—are attributable to what they ambiguously call 'natural causes'. Others still maintain that everything is referable to the interest and guidance of the Churchmen, and yet others—and probably with the greatest measure of truth—believe that the whole of the developments pivot on the traditions of the masons and the craft guilds.

Of these opinions the first is negligible—no natural causes could explain the parallelism and unanimity in design which is so manifest in the national architecture of the mediaeval period. The second and third views, however, call for more serious consideration, and may be dealt with as follows:

I. *The Churchmen theory.*

The original root of the Churchmen-builder theory is to be found in a book written as long since as 1877 by the Comte de Montalembert, *Les Moines d'Occident.* In that work, issued with a papal benediction, the Comte unhesitatingly affirmed that the monks were the only builders of mediaeval times, and he supported his theory by erroneous, if not even wilful, misconstructions of various early records. He elaborated his statements with entirely fantastic embellishments. Amongst other things, he said that the abbots not only drew plans, but supervised and directed work and, in some instances, even participated in the labours; that the monks sang psalms as they worked and that they only laid aside their trowels to perform the offices in the church. These are the words of Montalembert, vol. vi, p. 246.[1]

> 'Quand nous disons que les innombrables églises monastiques, répandues sur la surface de l'Europe entière, furent construites par les moines, il faut entendre l'assertion dans le sens littéral. Ils furent, en effet, non seulement les architectes, mais encore les maçons de leurs édifices: après avoir dressé leurs plans, dont la noble et savante ordonnance excite encore notre admiration, ils les exécutaient de leurs propres mains, et, en général, sans le secours d'ouvriers étranges[2] . . .'

The antiquarian and historical world of his day and for long years afterwards accepted these statements at their face value and without question, and it is only in recent years, the last decade or so, that they have been seriously criticized and their errors exposed. Dr. G. G. Coulton of Cambridge, Dr. A. Hamilton Thompson of Leeds, and others[3] have not only gone to the sources quoted by Montalembert and have revealed their truer meanings, and in almost every case

---

[1] Or in *Blackwood Trans.* (1879), vol. i, p. 218.

[2] Cela est expressément constaté dans la vie de saint Ethelwold, moine et évêque de Winchester. Act. SS.O.B., saec. v, p. 618.

[3] In 1923 L. F. Salzmann's *English Industries of the Middle Ages*; in 1928 Prof. G. G. Coulton's *Art and the Reformation*; and various writings by Prof. A. Hamilton Thompson have from time to time appeared. These writers, and particularly the last two, are the foremost leaders in mediaeval research and have contributed more authoritatively than any one else to the subject of the mediaeval builder. The latest book on the subject, R. E. Swartwout's *The Monastic Craftsman*, has only just been issued and is of distinct value. Besides these, Martin S. Briggs has published *The History of the Building Crafts* and *The Architect in History*; neither adds very much to what was known on the subject, and although they have some interest as a collation of known matter, their deductions are frequently unsound.

these entirely traverse the Comte's statements, but they have discovered other records which contravert his views. It almost seems
that the primary object with which the Comte wrote his book was,
like the writings of many of the early chroniclers, for the glorification
of the Church, even at the expense of historical fact.

It therefore appears that when the Comte states that the 'in-
nombrables églises monastiques . . . de l'Europe furent construites
par les moines' and that 'l'assertion (est) dans le sens littéral', he is
saying something which is absolutely untrue and unsupportable.
Unfortunately, however, his misleadings were followed. A. H.
Springer of Bonn—though with a reservation as to date—added:

> 'all . . . are agreed upon one point, namely that until the thir-
> teenth century all building work, painting and carving is due
> to the industry and skill of the monks alone'.[1]

This also fails in fact. Amongst other evidences Professor Springer
had apparently not considered the chronicle of Gervase of Canterbury concerning the twelfth-century work there of William of Sens
and William the Englishman.[2]

Still continuing along this *via erratica* later writers followed and the
wild tradition was perpetuated and spread until modern research
and scholarship swept it whither all such fantastic misrepresentations
are finally due.

To-day, however, the claim for the ecclesiastics of the design and
execution of actual work having been at long length abandoned,
another and certainly more plausible theory is advanced,[3] namely
that *style* dissemination is at least due to the Church. It is therefore
now suggested that as the Church fostered the arts in the Middle Ages,
and as architecture was the chief and most necessary of them, it must
be accredited with design—or style—developments. It is quite true
that the Church did patronize the arts and encouraged the practice
of many forms of art, but any actual practical participation therein
was confined within its own fellowship, save for a few specially
cited instances on the peculiar occasions of which its own chroniclers
specially commented. Apart from that, it neither designed nor
executed architectural works, nor did it follow up any sequence in
art development.[4]

[1] *De Artificibus Monachiis et Laicis Medii Aevi*, Bonn, 1861. But Springer's
further investigations, as noted therein, go far to prove exactly the opposite.

[2] See my *Med. Builder*, The Birm. Archaeol. Society's Trans., vol. xlviii,
pp. 19–21.

[3] It was seriously cited in the discussion after the original paper had been read.

[4] It is manifestly impossible within the limits of a paper such as this to
discuss the extent to which the monks participated in the arts. Probably their

In actual building works it of course provided conspicuous examples, which were to be seen and known of all men, and particularly of the building men. And it is because these examples could be, and they say were, copied that the Churchmen theorists maintain their revised case.

That copying was practised is not to be denied, indeed, quite the contrary, for frequent instances are known of definite undertakings by contract to do certain work like or 'after the pattern of' this or that existing example. Most of these instances, however, are of fifteenth-century date. For example, in the contract dated in 1426 for the tower of Walberswick Church (Suffolk) there were definite provisions that its general form should be as that of the church at Dunstale (*Dunwich*) and its west door and window as at Halesworth;[1] or that for rebuilding the cross at Coventry in 1542 which was 'to be in form fashion and due proportion in all points of a cross . . . in the town of Abingdon'.[2] The only instance of earlier date is that concerning the chapel at Windsor Castle, part of which in 1243 was directed to be built with a high wooden roof like that recently constructed at Lichfield.[3]

But is a claim tenable that such instances as these, even if there were many, really influenced the art of architecture as a whole in any appreciable way? It may certainly account for a measure of similarity in local works, but it is incredible that the general evolution of national architecture should rest on so insufficient and withal so erratic a basis, or that it should be in any comprehensive way affected by what this or that individual mason chose to copy or was directed to take as a copy for new works? Plagiarism, even if extensively practised, can never be seriously advanced as explanatory of the developments and widespread parallelism in architectural design throughout this or any other country.

Consider for a moment the fact that in England during the second and third quarters of the twelfth century there were some forty or fifty more or less important buildings in progress in the north; in the south there were others, and also in the east and west. In all of them there is very distinct similarity of features. At that time all

actual working contact with any of them was very much less than some enthusiastic exponents declare. In Mr. Swartwout's book, already cited, the whole question is very exhaustively dealt with and he shows with great clarity the true facts of the case.

[1] *Hist. of the Submerged Town of Dunwich*, T. Gardner (1754), p. 157.

[2] Dugdale, *Warwickshire*, vol. i, p. 145.

[3] Capella Regis Windesor' . . . 'et fieri faciat ibidem cumulum altum ligneum ad modum cumuli novi operis Lichfeld.' Close Roll, 27 Hen. III, m. 5.

work was of the Romanesque type, but as the thirteenth century opened and advanced and alterations, enlargements, or rebuildings after fires necessitated new efforts, they were then invariably treated according to the manner current at the later date. What accounted for the change in style? Who directed it? The only answer to such questions is to be found in the whole story of architectural evolution, the results of which were certainly not reached by any process of copying, however successful; copying merely perpetuates the forms it reproduces, makes no advance, originates no new ideas.

The copying theory, therefore, seems altogether inadequate as an explanation of the development in the styles, and some other and more sufficient reason is needed. And this is surely to be found in the craft-guild system and the master-masons, and no other proposition so fully covers the question.

II. *The Masons and the Craft-guilds.*

Let the pros and cons of the question, so far as English records go, be briefly considered:

(i) First the objectors to the guild system arguments say that there are no substantial and satisfying records, and that any references to *lodges* as guild appointments in connexion with building operations merely refer to sheds used by workmen as shelters or for the storage of their tools and materials and do not imply private apartments for special proceedings, secret or otherwise.

The reply to this is, first, that the references to mason guilds, 'general assemblies and confederacies', and the town and monastic regulations concerning them, of which there is a number of instances[1] though of late date, certainly imply very clearly the existence of guilds, *not as of merely recent formation*, but as established institutions. Besides this the analogy to continental guilds[2], records of which are frequent and full, cannot be ignored: England must unquestionably have had similar institutions, though the chroniclers have so unanimously ignored both them and the actual workers in their records of church building events. Further, the recorded rules, though also of late date, must have concerned organizations already well recognized. These rules refer to lodges, to their masters and wardens, to apprentices and journeymen, and to the ordinations to be

---

[1] The controls of London, York, and Coventry, and of the monasteries of York or Exeter are examples, as well as the regulations made by Henry VI interdicting the assemblies, though these were later modified or withdrawn.

[2] Cf. Coulton, *Art and the Reformation*, chap. v.

obeyed under oath of secrecy. Surely such evidences as these cannot be lightly swept aside.

There are, however, definite references to lodges—*loggs*—of quite early date; for instance, the *logg* at Windsor Castle in the fourteenth century, which, having accomplished its purpose for the masons' use, was afterwards converted into a residence for the Canons.[1] A building of such pretence and suitable for such later purpose cannot be considered as being originally only sheds.

(ii) Then as to the statement that it was on the greater works of the Church that the masons learned their craft, in the main under the tutelage of the monks.

On this the very pertinent questions arise: first, is it likely that though the great works of the Church were undoubtedly of first importance as architectural examples, they could possibly have influenced the general development of style throughout the country? No doubt they had local influence, but surely not a general and far-reaching one.

And then where did the monks learn—if they did learn it at all—so complete a body of architectural design as to be able not only to design for their current proposals, but to lead the way from the more or less foreign Romanesque style of the twelfth century to the essentially English work of the thirteenth, or to carry that forward by the obviously sequent stages it evidences into that of the later centuries? Where, too, did they learn such skill in operative mason-craft as the works claimed for them exhibit?

The fact is that if in any way they had an actual hand in the works at all, it was chiefly as assistants[2] to skilled lay-workers, and in any case their services were confined almost without exception to the home works of their own monasteries. This being so, no one will seriously believe that even if the one local enterprise of their experience—for not often in the lifetime of any monk was there more than one great effort—could have taught them enough to deal with further works at home, it certainly could not have enabled them to influence the art of the whole country. Therefore it seems quite safe to aver that monk-taught and monk-executed mason-craft is nothing more than a fantastic impossibility, and, moreover, the records—at least

---

[1] 'unum veterem domum . . . vocatum le logg. pro Cementariis . . . predictum pro habitacione omnium vicariorum ibidem per breve Regis, datum xviij die Julij Anno xlj' (1368). Hope, *Windsor Castle*, p. 212.

1532–3: in the Windsor Castle Works Book charges are noted for clearing away the ruins of an old lodge used by the masons 'wyche Lodge ffyll downe by Reson off Wynde'. Ibid., mentioning Rawlinson MSS. D. 775, f. 110.

[2] Indeed this is frankly admitted in some records.

such general records as there are—when rightly construed, are entirely against such an idea.[1]

(iii) Then there is the contract question. The anti-guild exponents urge that this would have so much hampered the guild institutions as to have made their existence almost impossible. But would not this argument absolutely and finally shut out the monk-mason theory? No monk could have contracted to do work of any sort or, for that matter, have done any work at all outside his own monastery, save in the most rare and exceptional circumstances of which there are only one or two isolated instances.

(iv) Finally—sweeping along the whole gamut of the question— if all the trades had guilds, and they did even down to those of quite unimportant occupations, then surely the masons must also have had theirs. They cannot have been the single—and singular—instance of exclusion. It is altogether too flimsy a plea to say that because the masons were men whose work as a rule called them from place to place, no guild was possible for them because it and its members could not be tied, as were those of the other trades, to any particular place or town. It has not even yet been finally shown that guilds must necessarily have been so tied or *per se* could not exist.

Is it not quite credible that companies of masons could have existed, submitting to a master or warden, and have moved from place to place as circumstances or work required? The remarks as to 'ubiquitous bodies of freemasons' made by Street, writing on Spanish affairs,[2] or the 'imagined secret societies' which Professor Prior seems to ridicule in one place but to support in another, are beside the point. To quote Professor Prior more fully—for the opponents of the guild system must be heard at their worst—he said there was an

> 'esoteric clique of archaeologists who explain the mediaeval building arts as those of a masonic society with a *mystery* that gave the monopoly of architecture . . . an imagined secret society has to be improvised for it.'[3]

His earlier remarks frequently refer to mason-craft and its evolutions and the bases of its expression; he says on this:

> 'the importance for English art lies in the combined outcome, (of Cluniac luxury and Cistercian temperance) for it established the national expression of English masoncraft.'[4]

A later remark, however, seems to support the guild idea which he earlier derides; for, speaking of the decorated work, dated towards

[1] Vide Swartwout, *op. cit.*, where the question is argued at length.
[2] *Gothic Archt. in Spain*, chap. xxi.
[3] *Chapters on Eng. Med. Art*, Cambridge, 1922, p. 75.   [4] Ibid., p. 39.

the end of the thirteenth century and particularly mentioning that at Exeter, Lichfield, and elsewhere, he says:

> 'In a general way these buildings illustrate a shift of style from constructive competence to the furnishing dexterities which in their action as craft monopolies make the second chapter of the fourteenth century style.'[1]

But the great issue is, as the Professor says, that of 'the national expression of English mason-craft', and whether apart from some determining and correlated organizations it could ever have become national, or developed with the unanimity of expression it everywhere exhibits.

Summing it up the whole matter appears to resolve itself into a choice between collectivism and individualism, and all other theories, save that of the mason-craft guilds, seem to fall to pieces when the life-stream of architectural evolution is traced either from one end of it or from the other.

Professor Lethaby's latest reasonings are far more acceptable and to the point. He said:

> 'Architecture was ... a compound of custom and experiment, of superstition and ceremony. From the first it had a physical side and a psychological side and these were carried forward in the long stream of progressing tradition ... "mere building" has never had an existence.... When the ancient schools of building flourished everything made was in its own rank of one artistic kind ... old architecture was found out by men working in stone.'[2]

He also said:

> 'About the year 1000 a powerful and progressive school of building began to form in Normandy.'[3]

and again:

> 'Mature Gothic art was chiefly concerned in cathedral and castle building, in town development and Guild organizations.'[4]

> 'Gothic architecture was developed by craft mastery fostered in the Guild, it was found out in the nature of things by exploration; it was not a look of grandeur or correctness obtained by making a composition of borrowed features.'[5]

To quote Professor Prior again, and incidentally in a passage somewhat in conflict with the opinion in the previous quotations:

> 'One is often asked who were the "architects" of cathedrals. The

---

[1] *Chapters on Eng. Med. Art*, Cambridge, 1922, pp. 93–4.
[2] *The Legacy of the Middle Ages* (1926), pp. 59, 60.   [3] Ibid., p. 64 et seq.
[4] Ibid., p. 73.   [5] Ibid., p. 91: 'borrowed features', i.e. copied work.

PLATE XIV

The Guild Warden examining Candidates

From a 15th Century MS. in the British Museum

reply must be that the function of architect as a designer of buildings and a determiner of its forms of beauty, did not exist in any personality. The dictation of plans and dimensions was in the hands of the high Ecclesiastic: the business was the perquisite of the church underlings: the execution was that of a trained body of craftsmen. Between these the cathedral was built, but the masons had the best claim to the honours of "architects", or at any rate "artists" by their faculty of work.'

'It is clear that the mason's craft had created a special class of skilled workers in stone and the circumstances of mediaeval building by the time of the thirteenth century lifted them into the highest position for leading and regulating the process of construction. From the mason class were derived the "magistri" who, as at Canterbury, were put in charge of the works.'[1]

Remarks such as these very definitely support the guild or 'school' theory and despite some earlier and apparently hostile declarations of Prof. Lethaby, no doubt his long researches at Westminster produced his later and very obviously revised opinions.

When the thirteenth century was far spent a change in architectural development began to show itself, and as the fourteenth proceeded it rapidly developed until a check was put not only on art but on all else by the appalling ravages of the Black Death, which began in 1347, and through which more than a third of the population of England is said to have perished. That and the Hundred Years War violently interrupted the flow in the stream of architectural evolution. But so far as the fourteenth century had previously run, building work was of a sequent and increasingly 'decorated' character. More and more ornateness was *applied to* it, rather than *rose out of* artistic treatment of the main proportions. After the cataclysmic break, it was not until towards the end of the century, when prosperity revived, that a new expression or any further developments appeared in architectural form, and the so-called 'Perpendicular' school arose, and this was unchallengeably due to the influence of the Gloucester school or guild.

Here, however, the matter must be left and the choice remain open as to whether the affirmative or the negative is to have the major support, or whether the guilds *plus* the copying of precedents, as given by the monastic examples, will be accepted as a *via media*. To affirm for the guilds alone may even yet be unwise, but at the same time it is clear that the bases for hesitation seem to be rapidly disappearing.

Finally it seems necessary to revise the current ideas as to the

[1] *Cathedral Builders*, p. 58.

status of these operative masters and to attribute to them, and particularly to the master-mason, potential abilities and artistic appreciations very similar to those which to-day are ceded, say, to a great sculptor, to think of them not only, or indeed at all, as mere labourers in preparing stone or other materials, but as men of refined and artistic perceptions, men of education and station coupled with a highly developed executive skill. They were the Flaxmans, the Framptons, the Tofts of their day, men who not only designed work, but who put on the smock and took the chisel and mallet in hand and cut their art in the solid stone. Such were the great master-masons of mediaeval times. There were, of course, the lesser men and also those of the less important trades.

All the evidence, however, supports the claims of the master-mason and with him the guilds. He was the chosen man, and with the workmen, usually of his selection and always of his approval, the enterprises were carried out.

In the course of architectural progress after, say, the end of the thirteenth century, there came by degrees what may be called the *church furnishing* era, the period when the workshop provided the fittings for the churches, the statues, the tombs, screens, and other of their necessary appointments. These were not often made in the buildings they were intended to adorn, nor were they designed by either the master-mason or master-carpenter who had the chief works of the building in hand. They were designed by the master-workmen in whose shop they were made, in part by him and in part by his workmen and apprentices. So at length there came to be many masters—masters in all the trades—and individual experts came into recognition.

A CATALOG OF SELECTED
DOVER BOOKS
IN ALL FIELDS OF INTEREST

A CATALOG OF SELECTED DOVER
BOOKS IN ALL FIELDS OF INTEREST

CONCERNING THE SPIRITUAL IN ART, Wassily Kandinsky. Pioneering work by father of abstract art. Thoughts on color theory, nature of art. Analysis of earlier masters. 12 illustrations. 80pp. of text. 5⅜ x 8½.   23411-8 Pa. $4.95

ANIMALS: 1,419 Copyright-Free Illustrations of Mammals, Birds, Fish, Insects, etc., Jim Harter (ed.). Clear wood engravings present, in extremely lifelike poses, over 1,000 species of animals. One of the most extensive pictorial sourcebooks of its kind. Captions. Index. 284pp. 9 x 12.   23766-4 Pa. $14.95

CELTIC ART: The Methods of Construction, George Bain. Simple geometric techniques for making Celtic interlacements, spirals, Kells-type initials, animals, humans, etc. Over 500 illustrations. 160pp. 9 x 12. (USO)   22923-8 Pa. $9.95

AN ATLAS OF ANATOMY FOR ARTISTS, Fritz Schider. Most thorough reference work on art anatomy in the world. Hundreds of illustrations, including selections from works by Vesalius, Leonardo, Goya, Ingres, Michelangelo, others. 593 illustrations. 192pp. 7⅛ x 10¼.   20241-0 Pa. $9.95

CELTIC HAND STROKE-BY-STROKE (Irish Half-Uncial from "The Book of Kells"): An Arthur Baker Calligraphy Manual, Arthur Baker. Complete guide to creating each letter of the alphabet in distinctive Celtic manner. Covers hand position, strokes, pens, inks, paper, more. Illustrated. 48pp. 8¼ x 11.   24336-2 Pa. $3.95

EASY ORIGAMI, John Montroll. Charming collection of 32 projects (hat, cup, pelican, piano, swan, many more) specially designed for the novice origami hobbyist. Clearly illustrated easy-to-follow instructions insure that even beginning papercrafters will achieve successful results. 48pp. 8¼ x 11.   27298-2 Pa. $3.50

THE COMPLETE BOOK OF BIRDHOUSE CONSTRUCTION FOR WOOD-WORKERS, Scott D. Campbell. Detailed instructions, illustrations, tables. Also data on bird habitat and instinct patterns. Bibliography. 3 tables. 63 illustrations in 15 figures. 48pp. 5¼ x 8½.   24407-5 Pa. $2.50

BLOOMINGDALE'S ILLUSTRATED 1886 CATALOG: Fashions, Dry Goods and Housewares, Bloomingdale Brothers. Famed merchants' extremely rare catalog depicting about 1,700 products: clothing, housewares, firearms, dry goods, jewelry, more. Invaluable for dating, identifying vintage items. Also, copyright-free graphics for artists, designers. Co-published with Henry Ford Museum & Greenfield Village. 160pp. 8¼ x 11.   25780-0 Pa. $10.95

HISTORIC COSTUME IN PICTURES, Braun & Schneider. Over 1,450 costumed figures in clearly detailed engravings–from dawn of civilization to end of 19th century. Captions. Many folk costumes. 256pp. 8⅜ x 11¾.   23150-X Pa. $12.95

THE INFLUENCE OF SEA POWER UPON HISTORY, 1660–1783, A. T. Mahan. Influential classic of naval history and tactics still used as text in war colleges. First paperback edition. 4 maps. 24 battle plans. 640pp. 5⅜ x 8½. 25509-3 Pa. $14.95

THE STORY OF THE TITANIC AS TOLD BY ITS SURVIVORS, Jack Winocour (ed.). What it was really like. Panic, despair, shocking inefficiency, and a little heroism. More thrilling than any fictional account. 26 illustrations. 320pp. 5⅜ x 8½. 20610-6 Pa. $8.95

FAIRY AND FOLK TALES OF THE IRISH PEASANTRY, William Butler Yeats (ed.). Treasury of 64 tales from the twilight world of Celtic myth and legend: "The Soul Cages," "The Kildare Pooka," "King O'Toole and his Goose," many more. Introduction and Notes by W. B. Yeats. 352pp. 5⅜ x 8½. 26941-8 Pa. $8.95

BUDDHIST MAHAYANA TEXTS, E. B. Cowell and Others (eds.). Superb, accurate translations of basic documents in Mahayana Buddhism, highly important in history of religions. The Buddha-karita of Asvaghosha, Larger Sukhavativyuha, more. 448pp. 5⅜ x 8½. 25552-2 Pa. $12.95

ONE TWO THREE . . . INFINITY: Facts and Speculations of Science, George Gamow. Great physicist's fascinating, readable overview of contemporary science: number theory, relativity, fourth dimension, entropy, genes, atomic structure, much more. 128 illustrations. Index. 352pp. 5⅜ x 8½. 25664-2 Pa. $8.95

ENGINEERING IN HISTORY, Richard Shelton Kirby, et al. Broad, nontechnical survey of history's major technological advances: birth of Greek science, industrial revolution, electricity and applied science, 20th-century automation, much more. 181 illustrations. ". . . excellent . . ."–*Isis.* Bibliography. vii + 530pp. 5⅜ x 8¼. 26412-2 Pa. $14.95

DALÍ ON MODERN ART: The Cuckolds of Antiquated Modern Art, Salvador Dalí. Influential painter skewers modern art and its practitioners. Outrageous evaluations of Picasso, Cézanne, Turner, more. 15 renderings of paintings discussed. 44 calligraphic decorations by Dalí. 96pp. 5⅜ x 8½. (USO) 29220-7 Pa. $4.95

ANTIQUE PLAYING CARDS: A Pictorial History, Henry René D'Allemagne. Over 900 elaborate, decorative images from rare playing cards (14th–20th centuries): Bacchus, death, dancing dogs, hunting scenes, royal coats of arms, players cheating, much more. 96pp. 9¼ x 12¼. 29265-7 Pa. $12.95

MAKING FURNITURE MASTERPIECES: 30 Projects with Measured Drawings, Franklin H. Gottshall. Step-by-step instructions, illustrations for constructing handsome, useful pieces, among them a Sheraton desk, Chippendale chair, Spanish desk, Queen Anne table and a William and Mary dressing mirror. 224pp. 8⅛ x 11¼. 29338-6 Pa. $13.95

THE FOSSIL BOOK: A Record of Prehistoric Life, Patricia V. Rich et al. Profusely illustrated definitive guide covers everything from single-celled organisms and dinosaurs to birds and mammals and the interplay between climate and man. Over 1,500 illustrations. 760pp. 7½ x 10⅛. 29371-8 Pa. $29.95

Prices subject to change without notice.

Available at your book dealer or write for free catalog to Dept. GI, Dover Publications, Inc., 31 East 2nd St., Mineola, N.Y. 11501. Dover publishes more than 500 books each year on science, elementary and advanced mathematics, biology, music, art, literary history, social sciences and other areas.